Usability Evaluation Handbook for Electronic Health Records

Linda Harrington, PhD, DNP, RN-BC, CNS, CPHQ, CENP, CPHIMS, FHIMSS

Craig Harrington, MS, LMSW, CPHIMS

HIMSS Mission
To globally lead endeavors optimizing health engagements and care outcomes through information technology.

Printed in the U.S.A. 5 4 3 2 1

Requests for permission to make copies of any part of this work should be sent to:
Permissions Editor
HIMSS
33 W. Monroe St., Suite 1700
Chicago, IL 60603-5616
nancy.vitucci@himssmedia.com

ISBN: 978-1-938904-58-5

The inclusion of an organization name, product, or service in this publication should not be considered as an endorsement of such organization, product, or service, nor is the failure to include an organization name, product, or service to be construed as disapproval.

For more information about HIMSS, please visit www.himss.org.

Dedication

To Nikki, Jack, Craig, and Kelly—May your life find expression and meaning through the work you do and the people you love.

About the Authors

Linda Harrington, PhD, DNP, RN-BC, CNS, CPHQ, CENP, CPHIMS, FHIMSS, is Vice President and Chief Nursing Informatics Officer with Catholic Health Initiatives (CHI) serving their Texas region. In this role she is responsible for leading the strategy and operational initiatives for nursing informatics, leveraging technology and data to improve clinical and financial outcomes. Dr. Harrington is board certified in nursing informatics by the American Nurses Credentialing Center and as a Certified Professional in Healthcare Information and Management Systems by HIMSS. She is also a HIMSS Fellow. She is the Technology Today column editor for AACN's *Advanced Critical Care* journal and a member of the workgroup updating the American Nurses Association's *Scope and Standards for Nursing Informatics Practice*. Her work on safety of electronic health records was cited in the Institute of Medicine's 2011 report, "Health IT and Patient Safety: Building Safer Systems for Better Care." She has published more than 50 articles in refereed medical journals and speaks nationally and internationally on nursing informatics.

Craig Harrington, MS, LMSW, CPHIMS, has more than 30 years of experience in information technology working as a software developer, executive, business partner, and health IT consultant. He holds a Bachelor of Arts in psychology from the University of North Carolina at Chapel Hill and a combined degree in computer science, mathematics and systems design from the University of Texas at San Antonio. He also holds a Master of Science in social work from the University of Texas at Arlington and health informatics from the University of Texas Health Science Center in Houston where he is currently a doctoral student. His study on using a unified framework to dramatically improve EHR usability was presented at the American Medical Informatics Association national conference in 2011 and published in their proceedings. Mr. Harrington also worked as a pre-doctoral fellow and a graduate research assistant on the Strategic Healthcare Advanced Research Project – Cognitive (SHARPC) funded by the Office of the National Coordinator for Health Information Technology. He is a Certified Professional in Healthcare Information and Management Systems by HIMSS and a member of the American Medical Informatics Association, the Association for Computing Machinery, and IEEE Computer Society where he serves on the standards committee for engineering and management of websites.

Contents

Acknowledgments

Writing this book has reinforced the old adage that "life is a journey." Our journey started years ago in different professions but has brought us together in a field that we are both passionate about—informatics. With that in mind, we would like to acknowledge the following individuals whom we have had the privilege of personally learning from and who continue to inspire us every day. No words could ever express our gratitude for the generosity and excellence with which they shared their knowledge, passion and wisdom in informatics and, more specifically, usability.

Jiajie Zhang, PhD, Dean and Dr. Doris L. Ross Professor at the University of Texas School of Biomedical Informatics at Houston and Director, National Center for Cognitive Informatics and Decision Making (NCCD), Houston, TX

Constance M. Johnson, PhD, MS, RN, Associate Professor, School of Nursing and Community and Family Medicine, Duke University, Durham, NC

Muhammad Walji, PhD, Associate Professor, Department of Diagnostic and Biomedical Sciences, Director of Informatics, Office of Technology Services and Informatics School of Dentistry, University of Texas Health Science Center at Houston, TX

Dr. William Edward Hammond II, PhD, FACMI, Director, Duke Center for Health Informatics, Professor in Community and Family Medicine Biomedical Engineering, and Adjunct Professor, Duke University Fuqua School of Business, Durham, NC

Foreword

By Jiajie Zhang, PhD, Dean and Dr. Doris L. Ross Professor, School of Biomedical Informatics, University of Texas Health Science Center at Houston

August 10, 2011, was a historical day for usability. At the close of the market on Wall Street, the market capitalization of Apple Computer surpassed that of Exxon Mobil for the first time, and Apple Computer became the world's biggest company in market value. Apple's products, especially the iPhone, iPad, and iPod, are built on the systematic, innovative practice of good usability from the ground up. This historical event tells the world that "usability" could be more valuable than "oil"!

Health information technology (health IT), especially electronic health record (EHR) systems, lag far behind the technology of other major industries such as aviation, nuclear power, consumer electronics, automobiles, banking and finance, and e-commerce, not only in its adoption, but also in its meaningful use.

EHRs have great potential to increase healthcare quality, efficiency, and safety through wide adoption and meaningful use. This is the major rationale behind the national health IT initiative, started by President Bush in 2004 and strengthened by President Obama in 2009 with the $19 billion HITECH Act under ARRA, with the goal of having every American's medical records digitized by 2014. However, there are huge gaps between the status quo and the potential of EHRs. Usability is one of the major barriers to closing these gaps.

Although Safety-Enhanced Design, a major component of usability, is now required for 2014 Meaningful Use Certification of EHRs, there are still enormous challenges in disseminating usability knowledge to the EHR vendor and user community, in practicing good usability for old and new products, and in establishing a process to ensure good usability throughout the product development lifecycle. This book by Linda and Craig Harrington is a timely, valuable addition to the effort of disseminating and promoting usability in the health IT community. It is a must read not only for frontline developers and designers, but also managers, executives, and policy makers in healthcare. It also serves as a good textbook and practical guide for anyone who is interested in EHR usability.

Preface

This book was written for readers reflecting the membership of the Healthcare Information and Management Systems Society (HIMSS), a diverse group of people who have come together for a common purpose. That common purpose is best expressed through the HIMSS mission: *To globally lead endeavors optimizing health engagements and care outcomes through information technology*. It is the diverse perspectives, knowledge and expertise of the HIMSS membership that will enable the unique membership to successfully fulfill this mission.

A very simplistic analogy of diverse talents and expertise coming together to achieve a common purpose involves the violin. It is easy to appreciate the difference between a person who builds a violin and one who plays a violin; both rely on different knowledge and skills. It is only as a result of their combined talents that great music is made. Success relies on their complementary skills and an appreciation for the role each plays in producing a virtuoso performance. Throughout this book, you will see this theme of teamwork and interdependence as essential to the successful application of usability in the development and implementation of electronic health records (EHRs).

The book is written by two people with diverse talents and expertise, an IT guy and a nurse, who just happen to be married. For years we have understood very little about what each other did. Our jobs were different, the industries we worked in differed and even the languages of our respective professions were dissimilar. We never realized the intersection of our passions until we arrived at health informatics. Informatics is a relatively young field that involves, among other disciplines, computer science, information science, cognitive science, and domain knowledge, such as nursing. In informatics, our differences have become strengths as we challenge each other to look at problems through different lenses. Usability is certainly a common ground about which we have learned, taught, published and presented. This book combines our unique insights and represents a logical next step for us to collectively share what we have learned.

Chapter 1 provides an introduction intended to lay the foundation for the rest of the book by providing key definitions that include usability, electronic health records and users. While the definition of usability can seem academic, it is important for the diverse healthcare audience to appreciate the need to move from the more general definition of usability set forth by the International Standards Organization to the more specific definition of usability for electronic health records by Zhang and Walji. We have tried to explain how useful, usable and satisfying a definition by the latter authors trump the efficiency, effectiveness and satisfaction of the former when it comes to electronic health records.

Chapter 2 includes the commonly accepted principles of usability that help further illuminate the definitions explored in Chapter 1. The usability principles are quoted in exact text from the authors. Examples are provided to further explain the principles.

Having laid the foundation of what usability is in Chapters 1 and 2, Chapter 3 delves into what is meant by usability evaluation, which is the ultimate goal of the book.

We attempt to delineate two general types of evaluation, namely usability testing and research. Having experience in both, we recognize the need to differentiate the two so as to better appreciate what can be done with findings from testing versus research.

Chapter 4 discusses the unique case of usability related to workflow. This aspect of usability is called out as it is often cited as creating the most pain for end users. We seek to take readers from the more simplistic view of workflow as steps in a task to a more multidimensional, dynamic workflow that better represents the complexities of professional practice in health care. It is through truly understanding workflow that we can find significant usability solutions.

Chapter 5 describes several usability evaluation methods that are useful in testing or research. Instructions are provided for each method, as well as tools and tips for using these methods. The chapter starts with some of the simpler tools, moves into those of more moderate difficulty, and ends with the more complex and comprehensive tools. As stated in the book, the use of more than one approach is essential in usability evaluation—otherwise, key information on clinical practice is lost and solutions become insufficient to support the work of end users.

Chapter 6 includes a discussion on building a business case for usability. Whether from a vendor or customer perspective, business cases are useful in seeking approval for performing usability evaluations and garnering the needed resources. The chapter identifies key areas to include when building the case that good EHR usability can save time and money for both vendors and customers.

Chapter 7 discusses the future of EHR usability. We articulate the need for optimizing EHR usability today, as tomorrow will bring even greater challenges to EHRs and EHR usability. As the base and types of users expand their unique needs, the technology will exponentially increase as well.

This is a period of dramatic and rapid transformation in healthcare. For the industry to achieve its ultimate transformative goal of providing the right information to the right people at the needed time and place and in the most useful way to benefit patients, there is much work to do. We are convinced that EHR usability is the key to realizing this goal, allowing us to create products that are both a joy to use and that allow users to do their work more efficiently and with better results. This book is intended to provide tools, ideas and knowledge that will help readers improve electronic health records.

CHAPTER 1

Introduction

Usability is everywhere. Nobody describes this better than Donald Norman in his book, *The Design of Everyday Things*, first published in 1988, in which he notes, "Good usability should make it obvious to the end user what they need to do."[1] An example he uses that everyone can readily identify with involves door handles.

Figure 1-1: An Obvious "Push" Door Handle

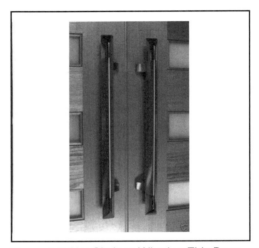

Figure 1-2: Not Obvious Whether This Door Handle Should Be Pushed or Pulled

Focusing on Figure 1-1, most people would know to push this door handle. No matter where they are when people see this type of door handle, they know to push on it and expect the door to open away from them. This is in contrast to the way people experience the door in Figure 1-2. When people confront this type of door handle, they often don't know whether to push or pull it. Users' eyes may quickly scan the door for a clue, or they may simply grab the handle and try to push or pull if the first action does not work. And, of course, sometimes it will be locked, making neither action work, thereby adding to the confusion and frustration.

While usability is everywhere, it may seem that awareness of usability is arriving late to health information technology (health IT), except perhaps to those who use it. Infusion pumps are a good example of how users recognize when something is usable or not. Anesthesiologists and nurses may have never heard of the concept of usability, but they can readily identify an infusion pump with which they like to work. They will tell you that it must be lightweight and have long-lasting batteries. They may also relate issues they have encountered, such as that in a crisis, one that is not preferred takes too long to power up or that the alarms go off too frequently, often for seemingly no reason. You may also hear about usability issues that, although not described as safety issues, can result in undesired and scary consequences. An example might be that it takes too long to search the machine's built-in drug library for a specific drug when, in emergency situations, saving seconds can save lives. Users may also remark that they cannot find a specific drug because it is not listed using the term they are most familiar with or terms that match the physician order. As illustrated by these examples and others, infusion pumps need a major infusion (if you will) of usability.

A superb example of poor usability impacting patient safety was provided by Ross Koppel and his colleagues in their book, *First Do Less Harm: Confronting the Inconvenient Problems of Patient Safety.*[2] As the authors tell it, a new physician was using a computerized provider order entry (CPOE) system to order a medication that she rarely prescribed. Once the physician located the medication, she found there were five different dosages in a list that read from top to bottom: 5 mg, 4 mg, 1 mg, 3 mg, 2 mg. Since the list was not ordered based on the size of the dosage, the physician pondered the logic behind the ordering of the list, thinking perhaps it was the most common dosing to the least common dosing, but she couldn't really be certain. The physician chose the 5-mg dose, based on the assumption it was the most frequent dose prescribed. As it turns out, the underlying logic in how the doses were displayed in the list was alphabetical order based on the spelling of the numbers, where *five* precedes *four*, which precedes *one* then *three* and lastly *two*. Who would have guessed the list was based on such an odd scheme? Certainly no user would, assuming that the logic was intended to help the users make the best choice.

Electronic health record (EHR) users are discovering that the obvious is not always so obvious. They are finding it difficult to access needed information from EHRs and difficult to enter data into EHRs in a timely manner. They are experiencing excessive demands on their memory, along with inconsistent and confusing information displays. Mismatches between the information in the EHR and clinical reality occur surprisingly often. Users are having to wade through excessive and unnecessary content. They are getting error messages that fail to provide clear guidance on what to do. They are finding words and acronyms they do not know. They are unable to search for what they need and when they can search, they fail to get the specific results they need. They are often unable to find a help function. And frequently, they feel inconvenienced or controlled by the EHR instead of supported in their work.[3]

How common are usability issues in EHRs? The short answer is that we really have no way of knowing exactly; however, significant numbers of usability issues are reported.[4] We do know that EHR usability can be evaluated and improved.[5] And we know also, from the Institute of Medicine's (IOM) report, "Health IT and Patient Safety: Building Safer Systems for Better Care," that poor usability is one of the single greatest threats to patient safety, and when it is improved it can actually improve patient safety.[6] We know that poor return on investment in health IT can be attributed in part to poor usability.[7] We know vendors express a deep commitment to usability but an array of issues in the vendor environment, such as competitive market forces and scarcity of both formal usability testing and experts in usability engineering, may undermine that commitment.[8] And we know that usability is not just an issue that vendors grapple with because customers frequently are heavily invested in EHR customizations and optimizations.[9]

While usability exists everywhere, this book focuses on usability specific to the EHR. The immersion of EHRs throughout the continuum of healthcare, the role EHRs play in healthcare delivery, and the overwhelming evidence of poor usability on widespread outcomes makes evaluating and enhancing usability a top priority. Improving usability is a process, not a one-time fix. To better understand this and the impact of EHR usability in the healthcare environment, a more formal introduction of usability is warranted.

USABILITY

Drs. Jiajie Zhang and Muhammad Walji created the accepted definition of usability as part of their framework specific to EHR usability. According to Zhang and Walji, "Usability refers to how useful, usable, and satisfying a system is for the intended users to accomplish goals in the work domain by performing certain sequences of tasks."[10] Their definition, focusing on the three major dimensions of *useful, usable* and *satisfying*, promotes an effective strategy for evaluating EHR usability, as each of the dimensions is measurable.

Usable refers to whether a system "is easy to learn, easy to use, and error-tolerant."[10] *Useful* refers to "how well the system supports the work domain where the users accomplish the goals for their work, independent of how the system is implemented." An EHR is *satisfying* to the end user when the end user finds it pleasing to use and anticipates using it in the future. *Work domain* is a concept that embodies the specialized skills and knowledge "where the users (seek to) accomplish the goals of their work."[10]

Usable is further delineated by Zhang and Walji as "learnability, efficiency and error tolerance." *Learnability* refers to the ease in learning or relearning the EHR. *Efficiency* denotes the minimal effort required to successfully accomplish a task. *Error tolerance* refers to the ability of the EHR to prevent users from making errors and help them recover when they do.[10]

Zhang and Walji compared their definition to that of the International Standards Organization (ISO) definition of usability, and the differences are worth noting (Table 1-1). The ISO definition of usability is the "extent to which a product can be used by specified users to achieve specified goals with effectiveness, efficiency and satisfaction in a specified context of use." *Effectiveness* is defined as "accuracy and completeness with which users achieve specified goals." *Efficiency* refers to the "resources expended in relation to the accuracy and completeness with which users achieve goals." Resources could include mental or physical effort, as well as time, materials or money. *Satisfaction* is the "freedom from discomfort and positive attitudes towards the use of the product." *Context of use* refers to "users, tasks, equipment (hardware, software and materials) and the physical and social environments in which a product is used."[11]

Table 1-1: Comparison of Usability Definitions

ISO Usability Concepts	Zhang and Walji Usability Concepts
Efficiency • Resources needed for accuracy and completeness	**Usable** • Learnability • Efficiency • Error prevention and recovery
Effectiveness • Accuracy • Completeness	**Useful** • Support of work domain
Satisfaction • Comfort • Acceptability	**Satisfying** • How useful, usable and likable the system is
Context of Use	**Work Domain**

Usable (Zhang & Walji) versus Efficiency (ISO). Key differences between the definition of usability by Zhang and Walji and the ISO are apparent when examining their respective concepts of *usable versus efficiency* and *useful versus effectiveness*.

- *Usable* and *efficiency* refer to the performance of the EHR. In the ISO definition, *efficiency* is one of the three key legs of their definition, while Zhang and Walji view *efficiency* as one of three necessary components of *usable*. The implication is that *efficiency* is not sufficient to make an EHR *usable*.

  For example, focusing solely on minimizing clicks to perform a specific task in the EHR as an effort to improve efficiency is shortsighted. Users may be dissatisfied with using the EHR application because the mental effort required by the user interface (UI) to find specific functionalities is burdensome. This could be due to illogical flow within or between screens, inconsistency in navigating, etc., making ease of learning, ease of use and error prevention deterrents to efficient use and thus usability.

- Error is another part of Zhang and Walji's *usable*, as error prevention and management capabilities will enhance users' ability to accomplish their work. The ISO definition includes error as an aspect of *effectiveness*, which does not fully recognize the value of error prevention and management in creating usable EHRs.

  To illustrate this point, consider that every time an EHR prevents users from having to deal with an error, the system is enabling users to continue working toward completing their task, thus demonstrating how error prevention and management are part of the performance of the EHR in attaining the end goals of *useful* and *satisfying* (Zhang and Walji) or *effectiveness* and *satisfaction* (ISO). Users are not typically skilled in knowing how to handle EHR errors (and do not want to acquire this skill either).

At a basic level, EHRs exist to make the complexity of healthcare more manageable to provide better and safer care. Healthcare is the point at which numerous rich and deep knowledge fields converge—technology, medicine, nursing, pharmacy, imaging, laboratory, social sciences, information sciences, accounting, asset management—just to name the more recognizable areas. In the context of voluminous content, efficiency is certainly important. However, a usable EHR that helps users focus on their work in a productive fashion is even more compelling.

Useful (Zhang & Walji) versus Effectiveness (ISO). *Effectiveness* is the ISO counterpart to Zhang and Walji's *useful*. "Measures of *effectiveness* relate the goals or subgoals of the user to the accuracy and completeness with which these goals can be achieved."[11] This portrays effectiveness as largely focused on the outcome of the user interaction with the EHR in contrast to the overall experience of the user. *Effectiveness* in this context does not provide a view as to whether the application requires users to deal with functionality that is superfluous and as such could complicate users' workloads.

As described by Zhang and Walji, *useful* refers to how well the EHR supports the work of the clinician.[12] The ideal *useful* EHR includes all the functions users need to accomplish their work. Additionally, the *useful* EHR will ideally only include those functions; that is, it will not include promotional information or information that other types of users might use but which is not relevant to the current user. For example, a cardiovascular surgeon requires different functionality than a gastroenterologist. And, as might be expected, what is required of an EHR to continually be *useful* changes over time, as knowledge and technological capabilities evolve.

Using the dimensions of *usable*, *useful* and *satisfying*, Zhang and Walji developed a framework, known as TURF (representing Task, User, Representation and Function), that is built around these four essential components that determine usability. The framework involves the following properties: (1) describing, explaining and predicting usability differences; (2) defining, evaluating and measuring usability objectively; and (3) building usability into the design of an EHR.[10] Their work is one of four projects funded by the Office of the National Coordinator for Health Information Technology (ONC) to develop relatively short-term quick-fix tools and long-term breakthroughs for health IT usability and workflow challenges. As such, acceptance of their definition and model of usability are encouraged.

While a comprehensive definition of *usability* is critical to discussions about improving EHR usability, a productive discussion also requires a clear understanding about what is meant by the term *electronic health record* and an explanation of how these two necessary parts form a sound strategy for analyzing and improving EHR usability.

ELECTRONIC HEALTH RECORDS

Previous terms and acronyms used to indicate what is now often referred to as an EHR include electronic documentation, computer-based patient record (CPR), and electronic medical record (EMR), among others. The two most commonly used acronyms today are EHR and EMR. Interoperability is the key distinguishing factor between the two, whereby the EHR denotes the ability to exchange data across different software applications and information systems.[13]

There are several definitions of *electronic health record*, and a good place to start would be the HIMSS *Dictionary of Healthcare Information Technology Terms, Acronyms and Organizations, Second Edition*, which includes more than 30 definitions in Appendix A.[12] The definition preferred by HIMSS is as follows:

Electronic health record. A longitudinal electronic record of patient health information produced by encounters in one or more care settings. Included in this information are patient demographics, progress notes, problems, medication, vital signs, past medical history, immunizations, laboratory data and radiology reports. The EHR automates and streamlines the clinician's workflow. The EHR has the ability to generate a complete record of a clinical patient encounter, as well as supporting other care-related activities such as decision support, quality management, and outcomes reporting.

Another definition of EHR that has withstood the test of time is that of the IOM. In a 2003 report titled "Key Capabilities of EHR Systems," the IOM defined the EHR as: (1) longitudinal collection of electronic health information for and about persons, where health information is defined as information pertaining to the health of an individual or a healthcare provider to an individual; (2) immediate electronic access to person- and population-level information by authorized, and only authorized, users; (3) provision of knowledge and decision-support that enhances the quality, safety, and efficiency of patient care; and (4) support of efficient processes for healthcare delivery. The report highlighted eight core functional areas of the EHR as health information and data, results management, order entry/management, decision support, electronic communication and connectivity, patient support, administrative processes, and reporting and population health management.[14]

One more definition worthy of inclusion that will resonate with those who recognize that data will drive the future of healthcare is that of the American Society for Testing and Materials (ASTM) Committee on Healthcare Informatics, Subcommittee on Healthcare Data Management, Security, Confidentiality, and Privacy. Their recently released standards focus on the data of the EHR stating, "An electronic health record is any information related to the past, present or future physical/mental health, or condition of an individual. The information resides in electronic system(s) used to capture, transmit, receive, store, retrieve, link and manipulate multimedia data for the primary purpose of providing healthcare and health-related services."[15]

While there are many EHR definitions, what is most important in defining the EHR is realizing that in the way the term *smart phone* is becoming a misnomer, the term *electronic health record* is also. A smart phone is not just a phone. It is a camera and video recorder, it allows access to one's bank, books, music, games, shopping, movies, and much more—all made possible through the digitization of data. Similarly, an EHR is not just an electronic record of one's health. Like the smart phone, the EHR is evolving to include more functionality, well beyond that of a record.

In addition to documentation, basic EHRs today include scheduling, coding and billing features, as well as some clinical decision support. In the future, EHRs built on more sophisticated and agile systems will allow real-time, self-service analytics for clinicians anytime and anywhere. Readily available and simple to use apps for patients will support them in better managing their health. And improved communication channels will afford quicker and often virtual access to healthcare and earlier intervention for health issues. All will have implications for usability.

Also like smart phones, every EHR has a user interface (UI). The UI is the face of the EHR where users interact with the application and manipulate its functionalities.[12]

LastName, FirstName	531787/31921	79y(06-Jun-1934) Female
Hosp-ICU-bed#		
ISOLATION:		**CODE STATUS:** Full Code
Allergies: Latex . . .	235/106.82/37.9	**ADMIT DATE:** 05-July-2013

Figure 1-3: EHR Patient Header

As a result of the UI, users have the options of clicking, scrolling or touching buttons, menus, drop-down lists, images, icons, hyperlinks and more.

It is tempting to view usability as a product of the user interface. However, it is more helpful to think of usability in a deeper sense, that is, as how the user interacts with the EHR. EHRs are more than a two-dimensional interface. There is an interaction between the EHR and the user's behavior and cognition, and the context. This is a critically important distinction to make as it provides the foundation to understanding why usability must be considered early in the development of the EHR.[16]

To better appreciate *good* usability, several examples of *poor* usability are described in the following paragraphs.

Patient Header. Take a look at the patient header in Figure 1-3. There are several usability issues. The color scheme makes it more difficult to read. Black text (both bold and not bold) on a gray background is challenging for clinicians who are reading the header in a fast-paced, sometimes dimly lit, environment. Did you notice the patient's age? You are not alone if you missed it! That is because the patient name and age, frequently used as patient identifiers, are at opposite ends of the header, making it a little bit more difficult for the user to read together. The ellipsis (. . .) following allergies means that there are more allergies but does not indicate where the other allergies are located, and there is no hyperlink to take the user there. More importantly, the format requires that all users know what an ellipsis is and what it means. While it may be commonly used in technical writing, its use is unheard of in clinical practice.

There are several numbers on the header that have no labels that identify them. The two at the top are the medical record number and the event number, consecutively. Not indicating what the numbers refer to makes it difficult if clinicians are asked to provide those numbers. The numbers at the bottom middle represent weight in pounds, weight in kilograms and body mass index. The lack of reference to these numbers heightens the potential for error. Clinicians using weight-based dosing may choose the wrong number, especially in emergency situations, creating overdosing or underdosing situations.

In the original screen for this patient header, "Allergies" is in red, which is curious, but not the actual allergen, "Latex." In contrast, "CODE STATUS" is not in red but the actual code, "Full Code," is. This is inconsistent as is the use of bold text and the use of capitalization.

Checklist. There are a lot of checklists in EHRs. The example in Figure 1-4 is about "Abnormals" of urine.

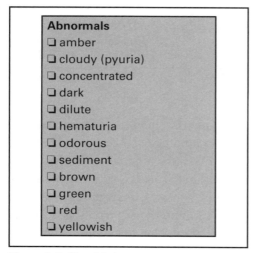

Figure 1-4: Checklist

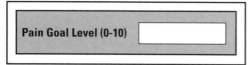

Figure 1-5: Pain Scale

A lack of logical sequencing exists in the list. The words are not listed in a hierarchical fashion or in alphabetical order. They are also not listed with the most common or critical abnormal first.

The words in the list also lack consistency in form and meaning. Notice that some colors are listed as brown, green, red, but then there is "yellowish." Why not yellow? And why is yellow or yellowish abnormal? What is the difference between red and hematuria?

Logic. Pain is measured on a scale of 0–10. In the EHR in Figure 1-5, clinicians are prompted to record a patient pain goal of between 0 and 10. Is a pain goal level something to be obtained or something to be avoided? Who gets a pain goal of 10? What is the logic to this prompt?

Duplicates. Creating different places in the EHR to document the same thing is problematic for several reasons. In this case, skin color can be documented in two areas—under "Skin" (Figure 1-6) and under "Cardiovascular" (Figure 1-7). It is worth noting that the attributes of skin color in the two lists differ, recognizing that one list has the addition of characteristics to color. "Grey" is on one list but not the other; "mottled" is on one list and "mottling" is on the other; and "erythema" is on one list, while "red" is on the other.

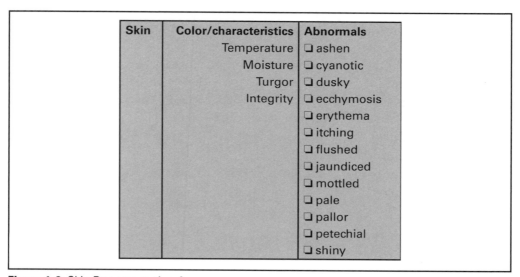

Figure 1-6: Skin Documentation A

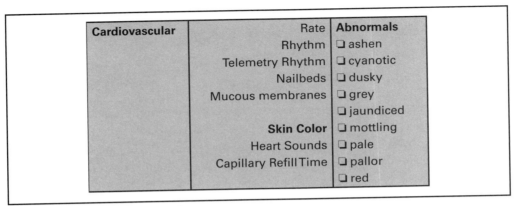

Figure 1-7: Skin Documentation B

Safety issues can arise when duplicate areas for documentation exist. Important patient data can be missed if clinicians are viewing areas of the EHR where the data were not entered—either because previous clinicians were busy or because the entering clinician is unaware of the second location where the data might have been entered.

Similarly, important patient data can be missed for quality reporting and reimbursement. In a particular EHR, one of the Centers for Medicare & Medicaid Services (CMS) core measures was located in two different areas of the EHR; therefore, nurses could document the core measure in one of two places. The problem was that only one of the areas populated the CMS report, resulting in inaccurate numbers for compliance with the core measure.

Cost is another issue with duplicate areas for documenting patient data in the EHR. There are costs to design, build and test two different areas of the same thing in the EHR and costs to correct the issue. Additional costs will be incurred to communicate the correction to clinicians. There may also be costs related to safety issues and lost reimbursement resulting from duplication.

Other. There are multiple other types of usability issues in EHRs. Some EHRs include checklists that allow you to choose all items when only one should be selected and vice versa. Sometimes users can inadvertently enter future dates for past events such as surgical procedures. There are ambiguities such as a physician order for "thrombus prevention measures" that does not list specific measures such as anticoagulation medication, which must be specifically ordered. Terms are found such as "functional rest positioning" that are not only unknown to clinicians but difficult to find if one searches the Internet for them.

These are just a few examples of the many, many usability issues that end users are dealing with in EHRs every day, 24/7. Researchers in one study detected 346 usability violations similar to those just mentioned in the area of clinical documentation by nurses in critical care; the detection method used typically identified only 60–75% of usability violations.[4,17] The study did not include the multiple flowsheets or the electronic medication administration record; it focused solely on clinical documentation in that one small area of the EHR.

As will be discussed later in this book, improving usability is *not* just about interface fixes. To better understand how users interact with EHRs, one must first understand the users.

USERS

EHR users come in many different stripes, including those more obvious: healthcare professionals from multiple disciplines; then generalists, specialists and subspecialists; and then clinical novices and experts and those in-between. There are full-time, part-time and *per diem* (PRN) nursing staff, as well as *locum tenens* or physicians working under temporary contracts, consultants and other temporary healthcare workers. Some users are computer natives; most today are computer immigrants. Some are technophiles, while others are technophobes.

EHR users are found in a variety of settings from hospitals to nursing homes to clinics to home health and, increasingly, within their own residences. Some cross among settings routinely while others tend to practice in a single setting. To further complicate matters, some users practice in different settings using different EHRs, sometimes on the same patients.

EHR users have different needs for the EHR. Some users will be managing their own health, while other users will be managing the health of others. There will be users involved in ensuring providers are meeting the ever-changing regulatory requirements. Others will be ensuring appropriate billing for services rendered. Researchers and safety experts, as well as quality improvement and risk management professionals will be using EHRs. All will be performing different tasks in different contexts. The unique needs of all of these professionals must be accurately attended to as users with diverse needs share the EHR simultaneously.

To further complicate matters, users' needs change over time. This evolution has been likened to Maslow's hierarchy of needs.[18] What the users expect from the EHR will evolve from satisfying some very basic and fundamental needs to fulfilling more advanced needs. More importantly, users will not move together *en masse*. Different users will have different levels of needs at different times.

EHR users require different information and displays that align with their cognition, workflow and decision making.[19] The goal is to make work easier for users, not add to it. Determining how usable, useful and satisfying the EHR is when being used in the context of the work environment and situation is the purpose of usability evaluation.[20]

It is essential for EHR vendors and health IT professionals to understand that just as usability experts are not users, users are not usability experts. When asked, users can offer what they think the EHR should look like and how it should function. More often users are comfortable sharing what they do not like and anecdotes about painful past experiences with EHRs.

Without sound knowledge and expertise in usability, EHR users are unaware of all the possibilities and best strategies for improving EHRs. Henry Ford said it best: "If I had asked people what they wanted, they would have said faster horses."

This is not to say that users are unimportant, because the reality is that user involvement is essential. To achieve the best results, their clinical knowledge and expertise should be combined with the knowledge and expertise of usability experts, designers, architects and programmers. Usability experts know how to translate what users want into effective solutions.

The fundamental question is *not* what does the EHR need to be able to do? Answers to this question focus on application functionality: the EHR needs to be able to order lab tests and to display lab results. Ensuring good usability of the EHR requires asking, who will be using the EHR, where will they be using it, when will they be using it, how will they be using it, and why? What do the users need to accomplish by using the EHR, and how can the EHR readily support these users in accomplishing their goals?

The bottom line is that EHR users deliver healthcare; they make it happen and they directly impact the outcomes, both clinical and financial. Users pay the price when they are expected to be productive but are using suboptimal technology. And this price is passed along to healthcare recipients, as well as to payers. EHR users want an information work environment that is sensitive to their needs and enables them to do a better and more satisfying job.[21]

COMMON MISCONCEPTIONS ABOUT USABILITY, EHRS AND USERS

Since people use their perceptions about usability, EHRs and people who use them to make decisions and take actions, it is important to recognize some common misconceptions.

Misconception #1: EHRs Are a Documentation System

EHRs are fundamentally huge databases that contain vast amounts of diverse, sensitive and complex data. This points to the important and undeniable trend that the data in EHRs are rapidly becoming the most critical asset in healthcare. These data are increasingly being used to improve decision making in patient care—both individualized and population-based—making accuracy of the EHR data vital. The quality of data is significantly affected by the usability of the EHRs.

Most EHRs today require a significant amount of data that is input manually. Users find it difficult to locate where they are supposed to input data. Even if they know where they must enter information, busy clinicians dread having to navigate multiple screens and long drop-down lists. Wading through crowded computer screens with unnecessary data entry fields often displayed using small fonts can challenge even the most patient users.

As human data are increasingly captured digitally through smart devices and automatically loaded into EHR databases in real time, usability will continue to be very important. How, when and where information is displayed to users will remain vitally important in their ability to quickly access it and use it efficiently and effectively.

Misconception #2: EHR Usability Is a Vendor Issue Requiring a Vendor Solution

EHR vendors have the first opportunity to employ enhanced usability as they develop their applications. However, EHR usability is not just a vendor issue and cannot be solved by vendors alone.[9] Granted, the bulk of the EHR lifecycle work is performed by EHR vendors who therefore have the greatest opportunity to provide excellent usability.

However, buyers of EHRs frequently customize their EHR in order to adapt it to enterprise standards or to match their unique workflows, or for other understandable reasons. These customized products are prime candidates for incorporating usability principles, but they are often limited by in-house knowledge and expertise in usability.

Misconception #3: Users Just Need More Training to Better Use an EHR

EHRs are intended to decrease clinicians' cognitive load. Alas, sometimes the best intentions result in unintended effects. For example, take the proliferation of icons to replace menu options. When there are multiple icons, many of which are hard to identify, similar in appearance or not intuitively designed, clinicians have to remember what they are used for. Similarly, when there are words or numbers that are not labeled, such as body mass index (BMI) or body surface area (BSA) on the EHR patient record header that are not labeled, users must remember what the numbers represent. When there are multiple areas where patient information must be entered, users must remember what the data entry screens look like, as well as how to navigate to them. In the absence of intelligent search functionality, users must remember the exact word or phrase to find what they need.

Misconception #4: EHR Usability Is Synonymous with EHR Design

While discussions on usability often include the word *design*, it is important to note that usability and graphic or visual design are not the same.[20] Drop-down lists are a good example. While drop-down lists can be great for interface designers in hiding a lot of content and making navigation in the EHR appear to be more clean and simple, they can be challenging and even hazardous for users. Selecting the wrong items or patient names in a drop-down list can and have led to errors involving wrong patients, wrong drugs, wrong dosages, and wrong drug route.[22-25] Usability is intended, in part, to prevent users from making mistakes.

Personal Story. *I went to an emergency department (ED) with a urinary tract infection (UTI). The ED nurse knew me and asked if I wanted to watch her document in the EHR, to which I replied yes. Since the system required her to enter my symptoms, she began scrolling through a drop-down list with dozens of items, looking for the precise phrase I had used, "pain on urination." She couldn't find it. She looked for, "pain during urination" and "pain when urinating" again with no success. I suggested she look for dysuria, the common clinical term. It too was not there. The drop-down list had numerous items to scroll through, making it a tedious search, and the lack of efficiency in finding the desired word or phrase was not lost on me. Finally, she entered the symptom as unstructured text into the EHR. The nurse then validated, "You also said you had low back pain" to which I replied, "Yes, on both sides." She was able to find that and clicked on the symptom.*

Fast forward a few months, the hospital bill came and I paid it. A couple of months later I received a letter from a third-party vendor the hospital had hired to determine if my back injury was due to an activity that may fall under workers' compensation. I spent hours trying to prove to this company that there was no back injury, my back was fine, and that the whole episode was about a UTI.

As it turned out, the phrase the nurse would have had to know was "painful urination." Equally important with this EHR, nurses would have to memorize all the exact words and phrases used throughout the EHR to readily find what they need in drop-down lists with numerous items. Too often these are called training issues. Yet this was not about training, and training would not have solved the problem, a problem that extended beyond my ED visit to my desk and to the desk of the payer, along with the cost of a third-party company to unnecessarily investigate. This was about usability.

The above story had to do with a drop-down list. What about an EHR with a search functionality? These are used to alleviate the issues with drop-down lists. Would this have helped?

Physician Story. A healthcare system implements a different EHR application than in the previous story. The EHR has a search functionality. A physician wants to order a lumbar spine x-ray and attempts to do so. Using any combination of the terms "lumbar," "spine" and "x-ray," or "x-ray," the physician cannot find the orderable using the search function. Why? Because the orderables were set up such that each x-ray began with "xr" and the user had to know that to find it. The term "X-ray" did not work. The entry had to be "xr lumbar spine."

So while the EHR had a search function, it operated like the drop-down list in the previous story. The physician had to know the exact term—not the exact commonly used term, or any commonly used term for that matter, but the exact term built into the search function, which was anything but common. This is not to say that search functions are bad; it depends on how they are built and, thus, how usable and useful they are.

One response to this dilemma was, "You just have to teach the physicians to search for x-rays using 'xr.'" However, there are a couple of issues with that solution. One, and perhaps the most important, EHRs are intended to reduce cognitive load for clinicians and serve as a memory aid, not as a memory generator. The approach to teach physicians to always use "xr" does not reduce cognitive load; it adds to it. It is but one more useless piece of information they have to remember until it is corrected—and then they have to unlearn it and remember not to use it. Plus, this was not an isolated case of a poor naming convention. There were others; others that would add to the cognitive load of today and the unlearning of tomorrow by clinicians.

Training issues are also associated with this solution. The nuance of "xr" adds to all the other needed EHR training content. And teaching this is not as simple as it may initially seem. It must be taught to all current physicians plus others who may be entering orders. It must also be taught to every new physician, faculty member, medical student, intern, resident, *locum tenens*, consulting physician, radiology technologist and technician, advanced practice registered nurse, registered nurse, nursing student, nursing faculty, agency nurse, traveler, and probably others. Who will coordinate to make sure all of this training gets done on an ongoing basis?

Both stories illustrate the far-reaching effects of simple usability errors that are readily preventable with sound usability evaluation. They also illustrate the impact of a very common design feature used in EHRs, the drop-down list, and the urgent need to make EHRs safer, easier to use and more useful to clinicians. And as Norman says, make it obvious to end users what they need to do.[1]

SUMMARY

The issues surrounding EHR usability are real and not isolated to any one EHR. Poor usability negatively impacts safety, productivity, adoption, costs and more. The goal is to make EHRs more usable, useful and satisfying. This book is intended to aid in this essential endeavor. The time is now, as EHRs play an increasing role in the delivery of healthcare. The next chapter, Chapter 2, provides additional insights into usability by examining usability principles.

REFERENCES

1.   Norman DA. *The Design of Everyday Things*. New York: Basic Books, 2002, 10.

2.   Koppel R, Davidson SM, Wears RL, et al. Health care information technology to the rescue. In: Koppel R, Gordon S. *First Do Less Harm: Confronting the Inconvenient Problems of Patient Safety*. Ithaca: Cornell University Press, 2012, 62.

3.   Zhang J, Johnson TR, Patel VL, et al. Using usability heuristics to evaluate patient safety of medical devices. *J Biomed Inform*. 2003; 36:23–30.

4.   Harrington L, Porch L, Acosta K, et al. Realizing electronic medical record benefits: An easy to do usability study. *Journal of Nursing Administration*. 2011; 41:331-335.

5.   Harrington C, Wood R, Breuer J, et al. Using a Unified Usability Framework to Dramatically Improve the Usability of an EMR Module. *Proceedings of AMIA 2011*.

6.   Institute of Medicine. Health IT and Patient Safety: Building Safer Systems for Better Care. Washington, DC: The National Academies Press, 2011.

7.   Kellermann AL, Jones SS. What it will take to achieve the as-yet-unfulfilled promises of health information technology. *Health Aff*. 2013; 32(1):63-68.

8.   McDonnell C, Werner K, Wendel L. *Electronic Health Record Usability: Vendor Practices and Perspectives. AHRQ Publication No. 09(10)-0091-3-EF*. Rockville, MD: Agency for Healthcare Research and Quality. May 2010.

9.   Harrington L. Usability of the electronic health record. *Health Aff*. 2013; 32(3):629.

10.   Zhang J, Walji M. TURF: Toward a unified framework of EHR usability. *J Biomed Inform*. 2011; 44:1056-1067.

11.   International Organization for Standardization. Ergonomic requirements for office work with visual display terminals (VDTs) – Part 11: Guidance on usability. ISO/IEC 9241-11. Geneva, Switzerland: International Organization for Standardization, 1998.

12.   Healthcare Information and Management Systems Society. *Dictionary of Healthcare Information Technology Terms, Acronyms and Organizations, Second Edition*. Chicago, IL: HIMSS, 2010.

13.   Johnson CM, Johnston D, Crowley PK, et al. *EHR Usability Toolkit: A Background Report on Usability and Electronic Health Records. AHRQ Publication No. 11-0084-EF*. Rockville, MD: Agency for Healthcare Research and Quality. August 2011.

14.   Institute of Medicine. Key Capabilities of an EHR System: Letter report. http://goo.gl/L4mKYg. Accessed July 1, 2013.

15. American Society for Testing and Materials, Committee on Healthcare Informatics, Subcommittee on Healthcare Data Management, Security, Confidentiality, and Privacy. *Standard Practice for Content and Structure of the Electronic Health Record.* E1384-07. West Conshohocken, PA: American Society for Testing and Materials. April 2013.

16. Juristo N, Morena AM, Sanchez-Segura MI. Analysing the impact of usability on software design. *J Syst Softw.* 2007; 80:1506-1516.

17. Nielsen J. *Usability Engineering.* Boston, MA: AP Professional, 1993.

18. Boehm B. A View of 20th and 21st Century Software Engineering. Presented at the 2006 International Conference on Software Engineering, May 20–28, 2006; Shanghai, China.

19. Armijo D, McDonnell C, Werner K. *Electronic Health Records: Interface Design Considerations.* AHRQ Publication No. 09(10)-0091-2-EF. Rockville, MD: Agency for Healthcare Research and Quality. October 2009.

20. Schumacker RM, Lowery SZ. *NIST Guide to the Processes Approach for Improving Usability of Electronic Health Records.* National Institute of Standards and Technology Publication No. NISTIR 7741. Washington, DC: US Department of Commerce. November 2010.

21. Zachary W, Neville K, Fowlkes J. Human total cost of ownership: The penny foolish principle at work. *IEEE Intelligent Systems.* 2007; 22(2):88-92.

22. Horsky J, Kaufman DR, Oppenheim MI, et al. A framework for analyzing the cognitive complexity of computer-assisted clinical ordering. *J Biomed Inform.* 2003; 36:4-22.

23. Zhan C, Hicks RW, Blanchette CM, et al. Potential benefits and problems with computerized prescriber order entry: analysis of a voluntary medication error-reporting database. *Am J Health Syst Pharm.* 2006; 63:353-358.

24. Bradley VM, Steltenkamp CL, Hite KB. Evaluation of reported medication errors before and after implementation of computerized practitioner order entry. *J Healthc Inf Manag.* 2006; 20:46-53.

25. Ash JS, Sittig DF, Dykstra RH, et al. Categorizing the unintended sociotechnical consequences of computerized provider order entry. *Int J Med Inform.* 2007; 76:21-27.

CHAPTER 2

Usability Principles

"Seek first to understand, then to be understood."

—Stephen Covey

To help readers better understand the concept of usability and users, this chapter outlines some of the commonly accepted usability principles (see Table 2-1). Some authors may refer to these principles as heuristics, rules of thumb or golden rules. They serve as the fundamental norms or rules of usability.

BACKGROUND

Nielsen's principles of usability, referred to as heuristics, are the most widely used and often quoted. Described by Nielsen as rules of thumb, the set of ten heuristics was derived from a potential 249 using factor analyses.[1] Nielsen is attributed with developing the usability heuristic evaluation technique.

Shneiderman's Eight Golden Rules of Interface Design were developed from experience and perfected over three decades.[2] Considered applicable to most interactive designs, the authors recommend validating and modifying their rules in specific domains, such as healthcare.

Zhang and colleagues derived their 14 usability heuristics by integrating, revising and expanding Nielsen's ten heuristics and Shneiderman's Eight Golden Rules, referring to them as the Nielsen-Shneiderman Heuristics.[3] It is important to note that their usability heuristics, while not specific to EHRs, were tailored for the health domain.

Gerhardt-Powals created what are called cognitive principles for improving human-computer interaction based on the opinion that many interface designs are not based on how humans process information.[4] Using ten cognitive-design principles extracted from the literature and applied to an interface design, four variables were measured and compared to two other interfaces that did not incorporate cognitive design principles. The cognitively engineered interface was found to have superior performance in reaction time and accuracy, lowest workload and highest user preference.

USABILITY PRINCIPLES

Table 2-1 provides a list of the common usability principles. The table is not comprehensive but does include some of the commonly used and often cited usability principles. The principles are not specific to EHR usability but most, if not all, can be applied to EHRs.

In reviewing the list and definitions of usability principles, four things stand out. The first and perhaps the simplest finding is the occasional redundancy or overlap. In contrast, there are also unique usability principles among the different authors.

Table 2-1: Principles of Usability

Principles	Definition	Referred to as:
Aesthetic and minimalist design[1]	"Dialogues should not contain information which is irrelevant or rarely needed. Every extra unit of information in a dialogue competes with the relevant units of information and diminishes their relative visibility."[1]	Heuristic[1]
Cater to universal usability[2]	"Recognize the needs of diverse users and design for *plasticity*, facilitating transformation of content. Novice to expert differences, age ranges, disabilities, and technological diversity each enrich the spectrum of requirements that guide design. Adding features for novices, such as explanations, and features for experts, such as shortcuts and faster pacing, can enrich the interface design and improve perceived system quality."[2]	Eight Golden Rules[2]
Clear closure[3]	"Every task has a beginning and an end. Users should be clearly notified about the completion of a task. a. Clear beginning, middle, and end. b. Complete 7 stages of actions. c. Clear feedback to indicate goals are achieved and current stacks of goals can be released. Examples of good closures include many dialogues."[3]	Heuristic[3]
Design dialogs to yield closure[2]	"Sequences of action should be organized into groups with a beginning, middle, and end. Informative feedback at the completion of a group of actions gives operators the satisfaction of accomplishment, a sense of relief, a signal to drop contingency plans from their minds, and an indicator to prepare for the next group of actions."[2]	Eight Golden Rules[2]
Consistency and standards[1,3]	"Users should not have to wonder whether different words, situations, or actions mean the same thing. Follow platform conventions."[1] Users should not have to wonder whether different words, situations, or actions mean the same thing. "Standards and conventions in product design should be followed. a. Sequences of actions (skill acquisition). b. Color (categorization). c. Layout and position (spatial consistency). d. Font, capitalization (levels of organization). e. Terminology (delete, del; remove, rm) and language (words, phrases). f. Standards (e.g., blue underlined text for unvisited hyperlinks)."[3]	Heuristic[1,3]

Table 2-1 *(Continued)*

Principles	Definition	Referred to as:
Strive for consistency[2]	"Consistent sequences of actions should be required in similar situations; identical terminology should be used in prompts, menus, and help screens; and consistent color, layout, capitalization, fonts, and so on should be employed throughout. Exceptions, such as required confirmation of the delete command or no echoing of passwords, should be comprehensible and limited in number."[2]	Eight Golden Rules[2]
Present new information with meaningful aids to interpretation[4]	"New information should be presented within familiar frameworks (e.g., schemas, metaphors, everyday terms) so that information is easier to absorb."[4]	Cognitive engineering principles[4]
Use names that are conceptually related to function[4]	"Display names and labels should be context-dependent, which will improve recall and recognition."[4]	Cognitive engineering principles[4]
Group data in consistently meaningful ways[4]	"Within a screen, data should be logically grouped; across screens, it should be consistently grouped. This will decrease information search time."[4]	Cognitive engineering principles[4]
Limit data-driven tasks[4]	"Use color and graphics, for example, to reduce the time spent assimilating raw data."[4]	Cognitive engineering principles[4]
Include in the displays only that information needed by the operator at a given time.[4]	"Exclude extraneous information that is not relevant to current tasks so that the user can focus attention on critical data."[4]	Cognitive engineering principles[4]
Provide multiple coding of data[4]	"The system should provide data in varying formats and/or levels of detail in order to promote cognitive flexibility and satisfy user preferences."[4]	Cognitive engineering principles[4]
Practice judicious redundancy[4]	"In order to be consistent, it is sometimes necessary to include more information than may be needed at a given time."[4]	Cognitive engineering principles[4]
Reduce uncertainty[4]	"Display data in a manner that is clear and obvious to reduce decision time and error."[4]	Cognitive engineering principles[4]
Error prevention[1]	"Even better than good error messages is a careful design which prevents a problem from occurring in the first place. Either eliminate error-prone conditions or check for them and present users with a confirmation option before they commit to the action."[1]	Heuristic[1]
Prevent errors[2]	"As much as possible, design the system such that users cannot make serious errors; for example, gray out menu items that are not appropriate, and do not allow alphabetical characters in numeric entry fields. If a user makes an error, the interface should detect the error and offer simple, constructive, and specific instructions for recovery. For example, users should not have to retype an entire name-address form if they enter an invalid zip code, but rather should be guided to repair only the faulty part. Erroneous actions should leave the system state unchanged, or the interface should give instructions about restoring the state."[2]	Eight Golden Rules[2]

Table 2-1 *(Continued)*

Principles	Definition	Referred to as:
Flexibility and efficiency[3]	"Users always learn and users are always different. Give users the flexibility of creating customization and shortcuts to accelerate their performance. a. Shortcuts for experienced users. b. Shortcuts or macros for frequently used operations. c. Skill acquisition through chunking. d. Examples: • Abbreviations, function keys, hot keys, command keys, macros, aliases, templates, type-ahead, bookmarks, hot links, history, default values, etc."[3]	Heuristic[3]
Flexibility and efficiency of use[1]	"Accelerators—unseen by the novice user—may often speed up the interaction for the expert user such that the system can cater to both inexperienced and experienced users. Allow users to tailor frequent actions."[1]	Heuristic[1]
Fuse data[4]	"Bring together lower-level data into a higher-level summation to reduce cognitive load."[4]	Cognitive engineering principles[4]
Good error messages[3]	"The messages should be informative enough such that users can understand the nature of errors, learn from errors, and recover from errors. a. Phrased in clear language, avoid obscure codes. Example of obscure code: 'system crashed, error code 147.' b. Precise, not vague or general. Example of general comment: 'Cannot open document.' c. Constructive. d. Polite. Examples of impolite message: 'illegal user action,' 'job aborted,' 'system was crashed,' 'fatal error,' etc."[3]	Heuristic[3]
Help users recognize, diagnose and recover from errors[1]	"Error messages should be expressed in plain language (no codes), precisely indicate the problem, and constructively suggest a solution."[1]	Heuristic[1]
Help and documentation[1,3]	"Even though it is better if the system can be used without documentation, it may be necessary to provide help and documentation. Any such information should be easy to search, focused on the user's task, list concrete steps to be carried out, and not be too large."[1] "Always provide help when needed. a. Context-sensitive help. b. Four types of help. • Task-oriented; • Alphabetically ordered; • Semantically organized; • Search. c. Help embedded in contents."[3]	Heuristic[1,3]

Table 2-1 *(Continued)*

Principles	Definition	Referred to as:

Informative feedback[3]	"Users should be given prompt and informative feedback about their actions.
	
	a. Information that can be directly perceived, interpreted, and evaluated.
	b. Levels of feedback (novice and expert).
	c. Concrete and specific, not abstract and general.
	d. Response time.
	  • 0.1 s for instantaneously reacting;
	  • 1.0 s for uninterrupted flow of thought;
	  • 10 s for the limit of attention."[3]
		Heuristic[3]

Offer informative feedback[2]	"For every user action, there should be system feedback. For frequent and minor actions, the response can be modest, whereas for infrequent and major actions, the response should be more substantial. Visual presentation of the objects of interest provides a convenient environment for showing changes explicitly."[2]	Eight Golden Rules[2]
Match between system and world[3]	"The image of the system perceived by users should match the model the users have about the system. a. User model matches system image. b. Actions provided by the system should match actions performed by users. c. Objects on the system should match objects of the task."[3]	Heuristic[3]
Match between system and the real world[1]	"The system should speak the users' language, with words, phrases and concepts familiar to the user, rather than system-oriented terms. Follow real-world conventions, making information appear in a natural and logical order."[1]	Heuristic[1]
Minimalist[3]	"Any extraneous information is a distraction and a slow-down. a. Less is more. b. Simple is not equivalent to abstract and general. c. Simple is efficient. d. Progressive levels of detail."[3]	Heuristic[3]
Minimize memory load[3]	"Users should not be required to memorize a lot of information to carry out tasks. Memory load reduces users' capacity to carry out the main tasks. a. Recognition vs. recall (e.g., menu vs. commands). b. Externalize information through visualization. c. Perceptual procedures. d. Hierarchical structure. e. Default values. f. Concrete examples (DD/MM/YY, e.g., 10/20/99). g. Generic rules and actions (e.g., drag objects)."[3]	Heuristic[3]
Automate unwanted workload[4]	"Eliminate mental calculations, estimations, comparisons, and unnecessary thinking to free cognitive resources for high-level tasks."[4]	Cognitive engineering principles[4]

Table 2-1 *(Continued)*

Principles	Definition	Referred to as:
Prevent errors[3]	"It is always better to design interfaces that prevent errors from happening in the first place. a. Interfaces that make errors impossible. b. Avoid modes (e.g., vi, text wrap). Or use informative feedback, e.g., different sounds. c. Execution error vs. evaluation error. d. Various types of slips and mistakes."[3]	Heuristic[3]
Recognition rather than recall[1]	"Minimize the user's memory load by making objects, actions, and options visible. The user should not have to remember information from one part of the dialogue to another. Instructions for use of the system should be visible or easily retrievable whenever appropriate."[1]	Heuristic[1]
Reversible actions[3]	"Users should be allowed to recover from errors. Reversible actions also encourage exploratory learning. a. At different levels: a single action, a subtask, or a complete task. b. Multiple steps."[3]	Heuristic[3]
Permit easy reversal of actions[2]	"As much as possible, actions should be reversible. This feature relieves anxiety, since the user knows that errors can be undone, and encourages exploration of unfamiliar options. The units of reversibility may be a single action, a data-entry task, or a complete group of actions, such as entry of a name-address block."[2]	Eight Golden Rules[2]
Use users' language[3]	"The language should be always presented in a form understandable by the intended users. a. Use standard meanings of words. b. Specialized language for specialized group. c. User-defined aliases. d. Users' perspective. Example: 'We have bought four tickets for you' (bad) vs. 'You bought four tickets' (good)."[3]	Heuristic[3]
User control and freedom[1]	"Users often choose system functions by mistake and will need a clearly marked 'emergency exit' to leave the unwanted state without having to go through an extended dialogue. Support undo and redo."[1]	Heuristic[1]
Users in control[3]	"Do not give users the impression that they are controlled by the systems. a. Users are initiators of actions, not responders to actions. b. Avoid surprising actions, unexpected outcomes, tedious sequences of actions, etc."[3]	Heuristic[3]
Support internal locus of control[2]	"Experienced users strongly desire the sense that they are in charge of the interface and that the interface responds to their actions. They don't want surprises or changes in familiar behavior, and they are annoyed by tedious data-entry sequences, difficulty in obtaining necessary information, and inability to produce their desired result."[2]	Eight Golden Rules[2]
Visibility of system status[1]	"The system should always keep users informed about what is going on, through appropriate feedback within reasonable time."[1]	Heuristic[1]

Table 2-1 *(Continued)*

Principles	Definition	Referred to as:
Visibility of system state[3]	"Users should be informed about what is going on with the system through appropriate feedback and display of information. a. What is the current state of the system? b. What can be done at current state? c. Where can users go? d. What change is made after an action?"[3]	Heuristic[3]

The second thing that stands out is the use of the word "user" in almost every definition. The significance of this cannot be overstated in distinguishing design from usability. How much of EHR development to date has leaned on design principles to the exclusion of usability principles? Chapter 1 of this book began with a simple example of good design but poor usability. The example is a door designed with a beautiful door handle but the user cannot readily tell whether to use the door handle to push or pull.

Lack of the word "workflow" in these usability principles is an important third finding. In the domain of healthcare, workflow is a critical consideration for usability that significantly impacts EHR implementation, user adoption of EHRs and the goal of creating usable, useful and satisfying EHRs. The word "workflow" is essential in any set of usability principles in healthcare, whether referred to as heuristics, rules of thumb, or golden rules, including a requirement for good workflow in relation to users, tasks and context.

The fourth or last thing that stands out, based on the other three, is the opportunity for research. Usability principles are fundamental to usability design and evaluation. The opportunity for researchers is to validate a list of comprehensive usability principles and associated definitions specific to the domain of healthcare with implications for EHRs.

VIOLATIONS OF USABILITY PRINCIPLES

To better illuminate the usability principles and the importance of using them in designing good EHR usability, examples of violations of the principles are described as follows.

Clear Closure. With clear closure, every task has a clear beginning, middle and end.[3] The panel in Figure 2-1 has no obvious way for a user to enter a new allergy or adverse drug reaction. There are no menu options, and clicking on the "Allergies / Adverse Reactions" header only changes the sort order of the listed allergies. To add new allergies, the user must right-click to bring up an option.

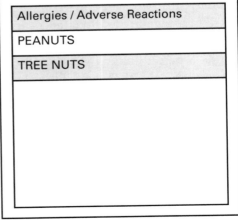

Figure 2-1: Lack of a Beginning, Middle or End

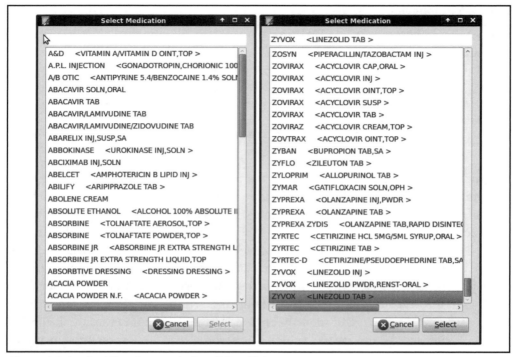

Figure 2-2: Lack of Consistency in Scroll Bar Sizing

Consistency and Standards. The size of scroll bars is expected to be consistent in providing a visual clue as to the amount of information that is available to be displayed. In the panel on the left in Figure 2-2, based on the size of the scroll bar, the 21 items from "A&D..." to "ACACIA POWDER..." represent about one third of the items available to be displayed. However, as the user scrolls down, the scroll bar shrinks in size as items are added to the display. When the user finally reaches the bottom of the file, over 6,500 items will have been displayed and the size of the scroll bar will have been reduced to a much smaller size.

Strive for Consistency. Defined as "consistent sequences of actions in similar situations,"[2] the two panels in Figure 2-3 violate this usability principle when users are asked to search on the left for an allergy and on the right for a medication. On the left, in order to see any options, the user must type three letters and then press the "Find" button, whereas on the right, the system defaults to showing a partial list—and as the user types a letter, the list gets filtered to show only options that start with the letters the user has entered.

Present New Information with Meaningful Aids to Interpretation. New information should be presented with familiar frameworks, such as icons, so that information is easier to learn and recall.[4] Icons are frequent violators. The syringe in Figure 2-4 may not be interpreted by clinicians as procedures but as medications. The icon for reports may also be difficult. Even if one could figure out that the basket represents "miscellaneous," it would be difficult to know what the word "miscellaneous" infers. Icons often require the user to remember what they mean and what actions are to be taken and what should be avoided.

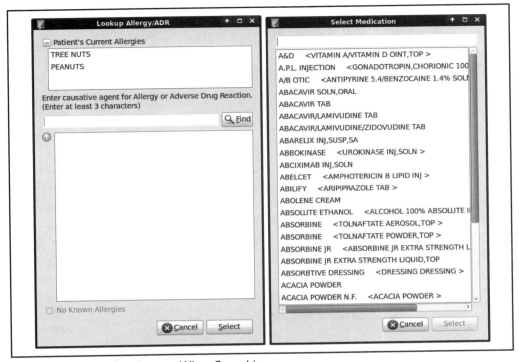

Figure 2-3: Lack of Consistency When Searching

Visibility of System State. Users should be informed about what is going on with the appropriate feedback and display information.[4] As can be seen in Figure 2-5, the information provided on the left is not interpretable. The user does not know if there are seconds, minutes or hours remaining. The image on the right provides the user with information so that he or she knows whether or not to engage in multitasking or to wait for the system to be available to them.

Figure 2-4: Unclear Icons

Figure 2-5: Unclear and Clear System Status

CONCLUSION

Usability principles help describe the concept of usability and provide guidance on the direction for improvement of usability in EHRs. The focus on "user" in the usability principles is advantageous to healthcare. Lack of the word "workflow" affords opportunity for improvement in usability principles specific to the domain of healthcare. Armed with a better understanding of usability, the next chapter explores usability evaluation.

REFERENCES

1. Nielsen J. 10 Usability Heuristics for user interface design. In Nielsen J, ed. *NN/g Nielsen Norman Group*. January 1, 1995. Available at: http://goo.gl/Gct4xS. Accessed August 18, 2013.

2. Shneiderman B, Plaisant C. *Designing the User Interface: Strategies for Effective Human Computer Interaction*. 5th ed. Boston, MA: Addison-Wesley, 2010.

3. Zhang J, Johnson TR, Patel VL, et al. Using usability heuristics to evaluate patient safety of medical devices. *J Biomed Inform*. 2003; 36:23-30.

4. Gerhardt-Powals J. Cognitive engineering principles for enhancing human-computer performance. *Int J Hum Comput Interact*. 1996; 8(2):189-211.

CHAPTER 3

Usability Evaluation

"What the usability evaluates: The problem of use."
—Stefano Federici and Simone Borci[1]

There it is—simply stated. EHR usability evaluation is about problems with use. It is not about design per se and it is not about interfaces. Usability is about use. Usability evaluation focuses on how well clinicians can learn and use the EHR to achieve their goals.

Before beginning a discussion on usability evaluation, definitions are in order. The literature is clouded with different terms, occasionally conflicting and other times overlapping. There are usability studies, usability testing, formal usability testing, practical usability testing, empirical usability testing, analytical usability testing, formative and summative usability testing, quantitative and qualitative, and objective and subjective usability evaluation.

A result stemming from the use of multiple and inconsistently used terms that is worth mentioning is the ongoing banter about usability testing and the lack of generalizability in some studies. *Generalizability* refers to the ability to apply findings of a usability evaluation to other EHRs, to other areas of an EHR not studied, to EHRs used in other settings, or to EHRs used by different users than those used in the testing. If the usability evaluation is not research, then generalizability is not a prime concern. Even if the usability evaluation *is* research, the ability to reliably generalize the findings depends on the purpose of the evaluation and the related research design (more on that later in this chapter).

Part of the underlying issue is the diversity of the individuals involved in usability evaluation who naturally view usability and evaluation differently. Researchers, as well as people from vendor and provider organizations, all have a vested interest in EHR usability but also have interests and perspectives that typically differ. Researchers want sound evaluations of EHR usability that are defensible and reproducible and that can ultimately yield significant and widespread improvements in usability. Remembering the adage that "A happy customer tells one person and an unhappy customer tells 12," vendors want products with such good usability that their EHR will turn providers into happy customers. And organizations want EHR solutions with good usability that is safe, satisfying to use and that supports the work of clinicians in improving patient and financial outcomes. All are valid and important needs.

The bottom line is that there is plenty of work to be done on EHR usability and everyone can contribute. We need usability to continue to mature and improve ways to describe and share the work underway so these diverse parties can understand and appreciate the work of each other. We also need to be efficient and effective in our usability improvement efforts, knowing that these systems are already deployed and there are numerous studies, reports and anecdotal data that usability issues are creating significant problems in the clinical setting.

The model for this book is that usability testing and usability research are different and fall under the more general topic of usability evaluation. Both testing and research use some of the same evaluation methods described in the next chapter on usability evaluation methods; however, the purpose and process under which they are performed differs. More importantly, what can or should be done with the results differs.

USABILITY TESTING VERSUS USABILITY RESEARCH

Criteria to distinguish between usability testing and usability research could not be identified through a search of the literature. Table 3-1 outlines an initial list of criteria in order to begin the dialog. As such, these criteria should be used as a guide.

Usability testing, as is used in this book, refers to activities or projects on a unique EHR being used in a specific setting or related setting. A unique EHR means one that has been purchased and customized or optimized to meet the needs of users in a specific setting. Related settings represent multisite organizations where the same instance of an EHR is used in multiple settings, such as multiple clinics or hospitals.

An example would be a provider organization that desires to improve the usability of an out-of-the-box EHR application to increase end-user satisfaction. While project leads may publish the process used to test usability along with their findings, the results are not intended to create widespread changes across multiple EHRs or settings because

Table 3-1: EHR Usability Testing Versus Usability Research

Criteria	Usability Testing	Usability Research
Purpose	To compare current EHR usability to established usability standards; To implement timely improvements in EHR usability	To generate conclusions which can be applied in or be predictive of similar circumstances; To generate new knowledge of EHR usability
Process	Test plan	Research protocol
Metrics	Tests against commonly accepted usability measures	Validates usability measures or uncovers new usability measures
Oversight of safety, privacy and security	None required	Requires institutional review board approval
Generalizability of findings	Not designed to be generalizable; Findings are specific to the usability project	Findings can be generalized depending on the research design used
Outcome	Improved usability of a unique EHR being used in a specific setting or related settings	Answer a research question or hypothesis

Table 3-2: Is the Project About Usability Testing or Usability Research?

Questions	Usability Testing	Usability Research
Is the project intended to identify and document usability issues within a single organization?	Yes	
Is the project intended to test a new usability standard or principle?		Yes
Are the findings intended to be used solely within the EHR of an organization?	Yes	
Are the findings intended to be used in similar circumstances across EHRs or organizations?		Yes
Is the project being designed to expand the knowledge of EHR usability?		Yes
Does the project involve greater than minimal risks to participants or protected health information?		Yes
Will the project lead to publication or presentation?	Yes	Yes

they are specific to the EHR of a particular setting or related settings. The results are intended to address specific EHR needs in the setting in which the testing occurs.

Usability research is also performed to improve EHR usability. Using a research approach that is based on the scientific process affords greater rigor and the ability to generalize findings to other EHRs, users and workflow. For example, a systematic review of studies on computerized provider order entry (CPOE) provides insights into usability issues from 19 studies.[2] Findings from these studies, which focus on usability issues such as alerts and drop-down lists, can be used to improve EHR usability by enhancing usability standards.

As an aid, Table 3-2 lists questions to consider when deciding whether usability testing or usability research would be most appropriate for the identified need.

USABILITY TESTING

Once satisfied that the purpose of the intended project is to compare current EHR usability to established usability standards or to implement timely improvements of EHR usability in a specific setting, the next step is to create a test plan.

Test Plan. The test plan serves as a blueprint for the usability testing, a communication tool for key stakeholders of the project and an initial indicator of needed resources.[3] The elements of the test plan are described next.

Executive Summary. This section is written last, as it summarizes the key components of the proposed usability test and includes the project goal, objectives, evaluation method, procedure, resources needed and timeline.

Team Members. Members should have the competencies to successfully complete the EHR usability testing. The team may include usability experts, clinicians, information technology professionals, safety experts and others.

Project Goal. Project goals describe the overall intent of the project. They are typically a broad general statement. An example would be to increase user satisfaction with the EHR or increase productivity of users when using the EHR.

Objectives. The objectives indicate what is intended to be achieved by undertaking usability testing. Collectively, the objectives indicate how the program goal will be

Table 3-3: Writing SMART Objectives

Specific	Measurable	Achievable	Relevant	Time-bound
Who is the focus?	Is the objective measureable?	Can the objective be accomplished in the proposed time frame?	Does the objective address the goal?	Does the objective propose a timeline within which the objective will be met?
End users	Amount of time it takes users to complete tasks X, Y and Z in the EHR	Specific time allotted (must be identified)	To increase productivity of end users	During usability test

accomplished. Objectives should be written using the SMART format, with SMART standing for *specific, measurable, achievable, relevant* and *time-bound.* An example objective: To identify the amount of time it takes users to complete tasks X, Y and Z in the EHR as described in Table 3-3.

Scope. A description of the usability testing scope includes detailed information on the EHR version/year, users, workflow, tasks, context, etc. If usability testing is limited to specific screens or areas of the EHR and users, such as CPOE medication ordering and hospitalists, that should be detailed as well. The phase of the lifecycle being tested should also be included. Another point to consider in the scope is whether the test plan will be executed again in the future to measure improvement after changes are made.

Method. It is important to describe the method used in the usability testing in sufficient detail so people reading the test plan can ascertain feasibility for use in their own setting. Important components of the method are described next.

Usability Evaluation Method. The usability evaluation method for the testing should be described so that readers can appreciate its ability to achieve the desired project goal(s).

Participants. The number and types of people involved in EHR usability testing should be described, including the rationale. Participants can include usability experts, end users, technology experts and others. Some may have experience in usability and some may not. Any required training to be provided prior to testing should be described.

Workflows. Specific workflows should be identified upfront. These may include those users are reporting as problematic, or they may be high-volume or critical workflows.

Context. The context in which the testing will be performed should be described including how well the context reflects the users' reality. Context may involve a busy, noisy or poorly lighted work environment or time of day.

Procedure. A high-level outline of the procedure should be included in the test plan. This can range from instructions provided to participants to post-test debriefing. The procedure should reflect the standard steps used for the usability evaluation method being employed.

Test Location. This section describes the setting in which the EHR usability testing will be performed. This could include a laboratory, clinical setting or other. The availability of the location should also be addressed.

Test Environment. The test environment ranges from the laboratory setup to the devices being used to the applications being tested. Each should be described.

Test Forms and Tools. Any forms or tools to be used in the testing should be described. These can include paper-and-pencil questionnaires or checklists, equipment such as eye-tracking devices or audio recordings, or structures such as two-way mirrors.

Usability Metrics. A list of metrics and definitions that measure the stated objectives of the usability testing project should also be included. For example, a metric might be efficiency that is defined for the test as how much time it takes for users to complete a specific task.

Analysis of Findings. The test plan should include a description of how the results will be analyzed, as well as how the analysis will be interpreted. For example, it is not enough to say that numbers will be added together. There must also be a discussion on how the sum of those added numbers can be interpreted in the context of the usability test.

Use of Findings. A description of how the findings will be used should be included. Potential uses may include recommendations for further usability testing or specific usability improvements. Opportunities to share lessons learned by publishing or presenting, internally or externally to the organization, should routinely be considered.

Timeline. The test plan should also include a timeline for activities with key milestones such as projected testing dates and data analyses. Again, this will enable readers to determine feasibility.

Resources. The usability test plan should also include a list of human, equipment and financial resources needed for the usability testing project to succeed.

Once the test plan is complete, a final check before release of the test plan to key stakeholders and the initiation of the usability testing involves alignment of the different elements of the plan. Table 3-4 provides an example of ensuring alignment of the project goal, objectives, usability evaluation method, usability metrics, analysis of findings and use of findings.

A well-developed test plan for EHR usability testing provides valuable information to project stakeholders, as well as team members. Thorough preparation serves to decrease problems from arising during usability testing. Once testing is completed, a usability test report is generated.

Table 3-4: Aligning the Test Plan

Project Goal	Objective(s)	Usability Evaluation Method	Usability Metrics	Analysis of Findings	Use of Findings
Increase productivity of users when using the EHR	To identify the amount of time it takes users to complete tasks X, Y and Z in the EHR	Keystroke Level Model (KLM)	Efficiency: Amount of time to complete a task	The median and range of time provide insights into user variation on amount of time in the identified tasks	Combining these findings with additional objectives on accuracy in completing same tasks may point to the need for a heuristic evaluation to improve task performance

USABILITY TEST REPORT

The usability test report outline in Table 3-5 is largely based on the template of reporting usability published by the National Institute of Standards and Technology (NIST).[4] Their template is intended to help EHR usability testers consistently and comprehensively report usability testing.

There are five sections to the report: Executive summary, introduction, method, results, and appendices. Contents of the template are outlined in Table 3-5. Not all sections are required for all usability testing and reporting.

Table 3-5: Usability Test Report

Section	Description
Title Page	Product and Version Tested: Date of Usability Test: Date of Report: Report Prepared By:

Table of Contents	1. Executive Summary
	2. Introduction
	3. Procedure
	    2.1 Evaluation Method
	    2.2 Participants
	    2.3 Tasks
	    2.4 Context
	    2.5 Procedure
	    2.6 Test Location
	    2.7 Test Environment
	    2.8 Test Forms and Tools
	    2.9 Participant Instructions
	    2.10 Usability Metrics
	4. Results
	    3.1 Data Analysis and Reporting
	    3.2 Discussion of Findings
	5. Appendices
	    4.1 Appendix A: Recruitment Screen
	    4.2 Appendix B: Participant Demographics

1. Executive Summary	• Name, version and type of EHR tested • Date • Location • Goal of the EHR usability test • Usability evaluation method used • Brief description of the test • Types of data collected • Major findings • Areas for improvement

Table 3-5 *(Continued)*

Section		Description
2. Introduction		• Name, version and type of EHR tested • Goal of the usability test • Type of usability evaluation method used to achieve the goal • Measures and metrics
3. Method	3.1 Usability Evaluation Method	• Description of the usability evaluation method that was used
	3.2 Participants	• Number of participants and rationale • Types of participants • Compensation provided participants, if any • Method used to recruit participants • Demographics of participants, such as gender, age, education, occupation, professional experience, computer experience, product experience and assistive technology needs • How participants were used in testing

	3.3 Tasks	• Description of tasks that were studied
		• Reasons for the selection of tasks studied
		  – Frequency of use
		  – Critical nature to users
		  – Most troublesome for users
		• How well tasks represent the purpose of the project

	3.4 *Context*	• Describe the context in which the EHR usability test is performed • Describe the context under which the user would perform the tasks being studied in the actual clinical setting • Discuss reasons for any variations in context
	3.5 Procedure	• Outline of the steps involved from beginning to end of the usability test • Ensure information is specific enough to be easily replicated
	3.6 Test Location	• Describe the physical layout where testing is performed • Identify who is present in the location during testing and what they were doing • Describe the environment in terms of lighting, noise, temperature, etc.

Table 3-5 *(Continued)*

Section	Description	
3. Method *(continued)*	3.7 Test Environment	• Describe facility where testing occurred • Identify computer type used and operating system running • Identify platform application running on and database type (train, test, etc.), as well as connection (LAN, local area network; WAN, wide area network, etc.) • Describe screen display, size, resolution, color settings, font, font size • Describe how participants interacted with the computer, i.e. used mouse, touch screen, stylus, etc.

	3.8 Test Forms and Tools	• Describe any documents or instruments used, including how they were used
		  – Moderator's guide
		  – Questionnaires
		  – Checklists
		  – Video
		  – Eye-tracking devices
		• Include copies in the Appendix

	3.9 Participant Instructions	• Describe instructions provided to participants • Describe any demonstrations that were given to participants
	3.10 Usability Metrics	• Identify measures studied • Describe what metrics were used for each measure
4. Results	4.1 Data Analysis and Reporting	• When possible, summarize data in tables and provide narrative explanations • Identify any data that were excluded and why • Identify any issues that could have affected data collection and interpretation of results
	4.2 Discussion of Findings	• Describe interpretation of findings • Identify limitations to the interpretation of the findings, such as differences in context between testing and reality
5. Appendices	5.1 Examples	• Recruitment screen—method used to select participants • Participant demographics • Copy of moderator's guide (if used) • Copy of tools, forms or questionnaires used • Copy of incentive receipt and acknowledgment form (if incentives for participants was used)

Item 3.4, "Context," under the Method section was added and was not included in the NIST document. It is recommended that usability tests be conducted with representative users under realistic contexts.[5] The findings of the usability test should include

a statement about how similar or different the context was between testing and actual use.

Also worth noting is the topic of incentives for participants. Consideration should be given as to the potential impact incentives may have on the performance of participants and how this may impact findings.

It is important to describe the usability testing in sufficient detail in reports so that people considering using the findings in their organization will know how well the usability test fits with their EHR, users, workflow and context, and what might need to be examined in advance. Lastly, the usability testing report should be written in past tense, describing events that have already occurred.

Effectively using the test plan and reporting tools promotes optimal outcomes for a comprehensive usability testing project. When the purposes of the usability project exceed those of usability testing better fitting the purposes of usability research, the unique tools to develop, implement and report are needed and are outlined next.

USABILITY RESEARCH

Federal regulations define research as "a systematic investigation, including research development, testing and evaluation, designed to develop or contribute to generalizable knowledge."[6] The purposes of usability research, previously described in this chapter, are congruent with the federal regulations. To repeat here, usability research is undertaken to generate conclusions, which can be applied in or be predictive of similar circumstances and also to generate new knowledge of EHR usability.

Usability research can be viewed as having four purposes: to describe, explain, predict and control. These areas are not mutually exclusive and some research covers more than one area. The area of focus is typically determined by what research is already available and has satisfied what purposes. In other words, if researchers are looking at a new phenomenon in usability, a descriptive study would be an appropriate beginning for providing a better understanding of what the usability phenomenon is, as that purpose had not been satisfied and is needed before moving to research that better explains the phenomenon.

Once the phenomenon is defined or understood, the ability to explain it may prove beneficial. An example would be that a certain usability issue is related to something. A research question might be this: Is alert fatigue related to the excessive use of alerts?

Usability for the purpose of prediction is important, yielding more actionable information than a descriptive or explanatory study. An example might be how many alerts or what types of alerts are more likely to result in alert fatigue. Understanding this would enable actions to be taken to further refine alerts. The last usability research purpose, control, could then be used to identify interventions that would work in preventing alert fatigue through better alerting.

Once it is determined that usability research is the correct path, the first step is preparation of a research protocol. Developing a research protocol affords researchers the opportunity to clarify their thoughts about the key elements of the research preparing to be undertaken.

Research Protocol. Similar to a test plan, a research protocol is a tool used to organize the proposed research project and prepare for a review. In the case of research, it may not be solely key stakeholders who will review the protocol but an institutional review board (IRB), whose sole purpose is the protection of human participants and protected health information that may be involved in the research. Table 3-6 outlines the elements of a usability research protocol.

Once the research protocol is complete and has been approved by all principal investigators and team members, it is submitted for approval by appropriate committees and/or leadership within the organization and then the IRB. One final check before submitting the research protocol to internal committees or leadership involves ensuring the process is in alignment.

Table 3-6: Usability Research Protocol

Title	Ideally,15 words or less, clearly describing the study	
Principal Investigator(s)	Name(s), credentials, title, and contact information for the principal investigator(s) responsible for the research project	
Research Team	Names, credentials and titles of members of the research team, such as usability specialists, clinical experts, user representatives, technology experts, consultants, etc.	
Location	Name and address of location where study will take place—hospital, clinic, health system, vendor, etc., plus city, state or region	
Background and Significance	Description of the need and priority for the study in light of current knowledge. Include prior literature and research, identifying any gaps in knowledge that the proposed study fills.	
Study Objectives	Primary objective—hypothesis or research question Secondary objective—additional hypothesis or research question	
Research Design and Methods	**Research Design**	Describe the research design and explanation of how the design addresses the study objectives
	Usability Evaluation Method	Describe the usability method that will be used in the study and how the method is consistent with the design
	Setting	Describe the setting and the availability of the setting during the time frame needed
	Participants	Outline inclusion criteria Outline exclusion criteria Describe withdrawal criteria Describe recruitment plans of human participants, if any Describe number of participants and rationale Describe sampling procedure (random, convenient, etc.) and justification
	Consent	Describe method for obtaining consent Describe compensation provided participants, if any State whether requesting "waiver of consent" from the IRB and provide rationale

Table 3-6 *(Continued)*

Research Design and Methods *(continued)*	**Electronic Health Record**	Describe computer device, type used and operating system
		Describe platform application running on and database type (train, test, etc.), as well as connection (LAN, WAN, etc.)
		Describe screen display, size, resolution, color settings, font, font size
		Describe how participants will interact with the computer device (i.e., mouse, touch screen, stylus, etc.)
	Data Collection	Describe any tools or instruments that will be used to collect data, along with their reliability and validity
		Include copies in the appendices
	Data Management	Describe how data will be handled and coded for computer analysis
		Describe where data will be stored and how it will be secured
	Data Analysis and Interpretation	Describe how data will be analyzed
		Describe how data will be interpreted in relation to study objectives
		Include power of the study, level of significance, or confidence interval, as appropriate
Potential Risks	Describe risks: Minimal risks are defined as risks having no greater probability or magnitude than those encountered in everyday life	
	Describe physical, psychological, social, legal, or other relevant aspects of risks	
	Provide an evaluation of the likelihood of occurrence and potential seriousness of identified risks	
	Describe interventions for preventing or minimizing risks	
	Describe procedures to protect participants' privacy and confidentiality	
Benefits	Describe expected benefits and the likelihood of those benefits being realized to participants, other persons, society at large or the science of usability	
	Describe why the risks to participants are reasonable in relation to the anticipated benefits of the research for the participants, other persons and society at large	
Limitations	Include any special considerations	
	No human participants (formerly called subjects)	
	No protected health information	
Results	Discuss potential application of findings	
Timeline	Provide a tentative timetable for the study identifying key milestones such as pilot, data collection and data analysis. Include estimated start day, anticipated duration of the study and estimated completion date	
Institutional Review Board Approval	Identify which IRB will be used	
	Include deadline for submission and anticipated date of IRB approval	
Piloting	Describe plans for piloting the study following IRB approval	
Expected Outcomes	Discuss how the EHR study will advance the knowledge of EHR usability	

Table 3-6 *(Continued)*

Dissemination of Results	Describe how the results will be disseminated in publication and presentation, including who will be lead author and order of other authors, plus any acknowledgments to be mentioned
	Discuss any plans to disseminate findings to policymakers
References	Provide a list of relevant literature citations
Appendices	Provide copies of forms, documents, tools used in the research
	Provide letters of confirmation from collaborating organizations, consultants, etc.

ALIGNING THE RESEARCH PROCESS

Sometimes people propose to do research that is descriptive in nature and then include predictive statistics and interpretation of findings as proving cause and effect. To avoid making these critical errors, be sure that each aspect of the proposed research is in alignment. For example, if the research question or hypothesis addresses relationships, then the research design should be a blueprint for testing relationships. The statistics used in the analysis of the data should be correlational statistics and the findings should be written in terms of the strength of the relationship. Table 3-7 provides an example of how each phase of the research process must be in alignment.

As can be seen in Table 3-7, the usability research is in alignment. The research question involves differences in tasks among physicians, which aligns with an experimental research design. The evaluation method is a task analysis and the statistic used, t-test, measures differences in groups of participants. The findings are reported as "no significant difference" and the conclusions refer to differences, or lack thereof, in tasks when using paper-based versus graphical-based systems.

The well-aligned research protocol serves as a solid foundation to perform the usability research and later to begin writing the manuscript for publication. Sharing the experience of a usability research project is vitally important to the advancement of EHR usability. Publications and presentations provide a worthwhile venue for widespread dissemination of findings.

Table 3-7: Aligning the Research Process[7]

Research Question of Hypothesis	Research Design	Usability Evaluation Method	Statistical Analysis	Findings	Conclusions
Is there a difference in ordering task time between paper-based and graphical-based systems among physicians?	Experimental	Task analysis	t-test	No significant difference in the average time it took participants to complete ordering tasks on the paper-based and graphical-based systems	Physicians make the transition from paper-based to graphical-based EHRs without increasing overall time to complete ordering tasks

REPORTING USABILITY RESEARCH

Journals publishing research manuscripts routinely have standardized author guidelines that can be located online. It is important to note that manuscripts can be submitted to only one journal at a time, and also that journals are increasingly requiring IRB approval numbers in research manuscripts for inclusion in the publication. Table 3-8 outlines a typical format for organizing content when submitting a research manuscript for publication; keep in mind that the specific formatting of the journal where the manuscript is being submitted should be followed.

Each journal's author guidelines will also provide specific instructions for the style guide to be used, such as *American Medical Association Manual of Style* or the *American Psychological Association Style Guide*. Style guides provide information on how to format the manuscript. For example, the style guide will provide explicit instruction on

Table 3-8: EHR Usability Research Manuscript Format

Cover Letter	The cover letter is intended to provide information to the editor and may include:	
	• Information on related publications or manuscripts submitted for publication	
	• Information on gaps in the literature filled by the manuscript	
	• Word count, excluding the title page, abstract, references, figures and tables	
Title Page	• Title	
	• Name, credentials, title, employer and contact information for corresponding author	
	• Name, credentials, title and employer of all co-authors	
	• Keywords (no more than five) for use in indexing the article in search engines	
Abstract	Typically, abstracts are restricted to a certain number of words, such as 250, and include the following:	
	• Significance or background: Summary of the literature in one or two sentences, demonstrating the need for the study	
	• Objectives: Hypothesis or research question stated in one sentence	
	• Method: Description of the study design, participants and measurements	
	• Results: Description of the main results, including levels of significance and confidence intervals as appropriate	
	• Conclusions: Author's summary of what can be concluded from the study	
Main Text	Introduction	Significance of the study
	Problem	Rationale or significance of the study and literature review
	Purpose	Hypothesis or research question and how it fills a gap in the literature
	Methods	• Setting
		• Participants, sampling, inclusion and exclusion criteria
		• Design
		• Usability evaluation method
		• Data collection and usability measures
		• Procedures
	Results	• Sample attributes or demographics
		• Results presented by hypothesis or research question
		• Level of significance or confidence interval as appropriate
	Discussion	• Findings in the context of other usability research
		• Include any limitations to the study that may have impacted the results
	Conclusion	One-paragraph summary of the main points in the manuscript

Table 3-8 *(Continued)*

References	References used in the manuscript, formatted and ordered based on the style guide for the specific journal
Appendices	Tables
	Figures
	Acknowledgments
	Funding

how to cite references in text or how to cite references in the reference list and how to organize the content in different levels of headings.

Many journals now have capabilities for submitting manuscripts electronically. The components submitted are likely to be similar to those outlined in Table 3-8. Again, the author guidelines will provide guidance on how to submit the manuscript.

CONCLUSIONS

Excellent usability does not just happen when designing an EHR. Architects and designers cannot just follow a usability checklist and expect great things to happen. Excellent usability results when leadership recognizes the value of usability; when the goal of excellent usability is a passion, not a pastime; and, when usability testing and usability research are used to ensure that the end users have a product that is exceptionally useful, usable and satisfying. The next chapter, Chapter 4, presents the unique case of EHR usability related to workflow as the number one cause of end-user issues.

REFERENCES

1. Federici S, Borsci S. Usability evaluation: models, methods, and applications. In: Stone J, Blouin M, eds. *International Encyclopedia of Rehabilitation*, Buffalo, NY: Center for International Rehabilitation Research Information and Exchange (CIRRIE), 2010.

2. Khajouei R, Jaspers MWM. The impact of CPOE medication systems' design aspects on usability, workflow and medication orders. *Methods Inf Med*. 2010; 49:3-19.

3. Rubin J, Chisnell D. *Handbook of Usability Testing: How to Plan, Design, and Conduct Effective Tests*. Indianapolis, IN: Wiley Publishing, Inc., 2008.

4. Schumacher RM, Lowry SZ. *Customized Common Industry Format Template for Electronic Health Record Usability Testing*. NISTIR 7742. Washington, DC: National Institute of Standards and Technology; November 15, 2010.

5. Schumacher RM, Lowry SZ. *NIST Guide to the Processes Approach for Improving the Usability of Electronic Health Records*. NISTIR 7741. Washington, DC: National Institute of Standards and Technology; November 2010.

6. U.S. Department of Health and Human Services. Code of Federal Regulations. Protection of Human Subjects. 45CFR46.102(d). Washington, DC: U.S. Department of Health and Human Services, 2009. Available at: http://goo.gl/W2KKn8. Accessed September 2, 2013.

7. Rodriguez NJ, Murillo V, Borges JA, et al. A usability study of physicians' interaction with a paper-based patient record system and a graphical-based electronic patient record system. AMIA 2002 Annual Symposium Proceedings.

CHAPTER 4

Usability and Workflow

*"As aircraft become more complex and attain higher speeds, the
necessity for designing the machine to suit the inherent characteristics of
the human operators becomes increasingly apparent."*

—Paul Fitts, 1947

Following this quote, Fitts went on to say that the addition of new instruments and devices in the cockpit actually reduced pilots' effectiveness by pushing tasks to the threshold of human ability. The answer was clear and it still applies today. Like aircraft, the increasingly complex EHR must fit the characteristics of the people operating it—characteristics that are immersed in the workflow of healthcare professionals.

When it comes to workflow, a common perception is that EHRs fit or even improve clinicians' workflow. EHRs are expected to simplify documentation and orders management, enhance interdisciplinary communication, decrease inefficiencies, remove redundancies, eliminate bottlenecks, improve care coordination and prevent errors. Sadly, ask clinicians today and many will tell you that EHRs have worsened their workflow.

As a matter of fact, authors of a 2010 HIMSS study reported workflow to be the number one EHR usability pain point for clinicians.[1] As such, it was deemed important to include a special chapter on the topic in this book, as workflow issues can be caused by poor EHR usability. Identifying the underlying cause of workflow issues is essential in finding the right solutions. But first, let's look at the meaning of workflow.

WORKFLOW

Unertl and colleagues performed a systematic review of the literature on workflow, uncovering 125 different definitions from 1995 to 2007.[2] Of significance to healthcare, the workflow definitions frequently focused on static processes that can readily be depicted in process maps or flowcharts, suggesting the primary view of workflow as linear and unchanging. Equally important, the authors asserted that in computer-supported cooperative work—as is typical of healthcare today—workflow is more evolving, changing and dynamic.[2]

A 2010 report on incorporating health IT into workflow redesign sponsored by the Agency for Healthcare Research and Quality (AHRQ) acknowledged the lack of a standard definition for workflow in healthcare.[3] Their conclusion was based on both a review of the literature on workflow, as well as an environmental scan of workflow issues related to the development, implementation, adoption and use of health IT. The authors reported one consequence of the lack of a standard definition to be substantial variation in workflow measures, making it difficult to identify the impact of health IT on workflow.

One of the commonly used definitions of workflow in healthcare refers to a set of tasks grouped into chronologically ordered processes, plus the people and resources required to complete the tasks and accomplish a desired goal.[4] In alignment with this definition are frequently seen methods to measure workflow using process maps, flow charts and swim lane diagrams. Also in alignment is the assertion in a National Academy of Sciences' National Research Council report in 2009 that health IT is designed primarily to automate tasks.[5]

When viewed as taking a patient history, transferring a patient to another area, developing a treatment plan or prescribing medications, workflow may look like simple tasks that are easy to automate in EHRs. Unfortunately, design efforts to date using this simplistic view have fallen short given the widespread and persistent workflow issues with EHRs in the clinical environment and the severity identified by end-user surveys. We will examine these issues next.

DIMENSIONS OF CLINICAL WORKFLOW

A convergence of evidence suggests a more complex, dynamic, multidimensional nature to clinical workflow than previously thought. Workflow tools and analyses that come out of manufacturing—where work processes are highly linear, static, redundant and easily measured—fail to meet the requirements of healthcare. Clinical workflow involves not only the physical aspects of work but also cognition, context, collaboration, communication, coordination and exceptions.

Cognitive Workflow. While clinical workflow is often mapped to physical tasks, it may be surprising to many non-clinicians that the majority of tasks performed by healthcare professionals are cognitive in nature.[5] That is, it is work that goes on in their heads, how they are thinking and what they are thinking. Cognitive workflow has been defined as the changing pattern of cognitive demands placed on clinicians as they perform the various component activities of a task.[6] Cognitive processes are active in diagnostic reasoning, decision making, interactions with patients and other healthcare professionals, as well as in interactions with technology.[7]

Using patient exams as an example, clinicians collect data about their patients by inspecting, palpating, percussing and auscultating the patient. That is the physical and observable work. During this physical exam, clinicians are continually and cognitively analyzing the data. The physical examination of patients is neither standard nor linear as clinicians delve further into different areas to confirm or exclude their forming impressions based on each individual patient presented before them.

Cognitive work involves perceiving, thinking, reasoning, remembering, decision making, problem solving, pattern matching and more.[8,9] Readily accessible, relevant

Medication Reconciliation			
Medications			
bisacodyl (DULCOLAX) EC tablet 10 mg Oral, daily as needed for constipation	Continue	Discontinue	Modify
captopril (CAPOTEN) tablet 25 mg Oral, 1 tablet every 12 hours	Continue	Discontinue	Modify
docusate (COLACE) capsule 100 mg Oral, 2 times daily, HOLD for loose stools	Continue	Discontinue	Modify
enoxaparin (LOVENOX) syringe 30 mg Subcutaneous, 30 mg every 24 hours	Continue	Discontinue	Modify
hydrochlorothiazide (HCTZ) tablet 25 mg Oral, 1 tablet daily	Continue	Discontinue	Modify
HYDROcodone-acetaminophen (NORCO) tablet 5-325 mg Oral, 1 tablet every 4 hours as needed for moderate pain (4-6/10)	Continue	Discontinue	Modify

Figure 4-1: Simple Medication Reconciliation

and meaningfully presented information is key to good usability supporting cognitive workflow.[8-10] EHRs that interfere with the cognitive work can adversely affect clinicians, increasing their cognitive workload, decreasing productivity, increasing their risk of error and lowering their satisfaction with the EHR.

Usability characteristics, such as ease of use, readability, standardization of information display and clarity of information, impact cognitive workflow.[8] For example, EHRs display lab results in an arrangement that may or may not support clinicians' cognitive workflow. They may be listed alphabetically by lab name or in chronological order of when the tests were initiated. In contrast, clinicians think about specific labs and trends related to the unique patient's condition, trying to mentally draw out relevant data from all lab data presented. The way information is displayed makes a difference in improving or worsening the user's cognitive work.[11]

A clinical workflow involving a significant amount of cognitive work is medication reconciliation. Figure 4-1 illustrates a simple view of medication reconciliation occurring prior to patient discharge from the hospital.

There are several opportunities for improvement in Figure 4-1. The alphabetical arrangement of the medications provides no benefit for cognitive workflow. The provider may first want to consider what medications the patient was taking prior to this hospital admission and what medications were prescribed during the hospitalization. Figure 4-2 supports this cognitive workflow.

The physician overseeing the patient's care during hospitalization may differ from the physician providing care for the patient in the outpatient setting. This is increasingly the case where hospitalists are used or when patients are admitted for an inpatient procedure. Until EHRs are interoperable across the care continuum and clinical decision support fully functional in supporting medication reconciliation, physicians overseeing the patient's care during hospitalization may be reluctant in advising patients to continue, discontinue or modify medications following hospitalization, especially when the medications being taken are self-reported by patients or family members and thus open to error.

Figure 4-3 provides another view of medication reconciliation supporting an evaluation of the patient's medications by drug classification. This allows the physician to quickly evaluate whether the patient needs analgesia, anticoagulation and other medi-

Medication Reconciliation			
Medications taken at home			
	SELECT ALL		
bisacodyl (DULCOLAX) EC tablet 10 mg Oral, daily as needed for constipation	Continue to take as prescribed by primary care physician.		
captopril (CAPOTEN) tablet 25 mg Oral, 1 tablet every 12 hours	Continue to take as prescribed by primary care physician.		
docusate (COLACE) capsule 100 mg Oral, 2 times daily, HOLD for loose stools	Continue to take as prescribed by primary care physician.		
hydrochlorothiazide (HCTZ) tablet 25 mg Oral, 1 tablet daily	Continue to take as prescribed by primary care physician.		
Additional medications prescribed during this hospitalization			
enoxaparin (LOVENOX) syringe 30 mg Subcutaneous, 30 mg every 24 hours	Continue	Discontinue	Modify
HYDROcodone-acetaminophen (NORCO) tablet 5-325 mg Oral, 1 tablet every 4 hours as needed for moderate pain (4-6/10)	Continue	Discontinue	Modify

Figure 4-2: Reconciliation of Home and Hospital-Prescribed Medications

	Filter by:	Drug Classification	
Medication Reconciliation			
Analgesic			
HYDROcodone-acetaminophen (NORCO) tablet 5-325 mg Oral, 1 tablet every 4 hours as needed for moderate pain (4-6/10) *Not to exceed more than 4,000 mg acetaminophen daily.*	Continue	Discontinue	Modify
Anticoagulant			
enoxaparin (LOVENOX) syringe 30 mg Subcutaneous, 30 mg every 24 hours	Continue	Discontinue	Modify
Antihypertensive			
captopril (CAPOTEN) tablet 25 mg Oral, 1 tablet every 12 hours *Maintenance: 25-150 mg q8-12hr; 450 mg/daily maximum*	Continue	Discontinue	Modify
hydrochlorothiazide (HCTZ) tablet 25 mg Oral, 1 tablet daily *Maintenance: 25-50 mg daily; 100 mg/daily maximum*	Continue	Discontinue	Modify
Laxative/Stool Softener			
bisacodyl (DULCOLAX) EC tablet 10 mg Oral, daily as needed for constipation	Continue	Discontinue	Modify
docusate (COLACE) capsule 100 mg Oral, 2 times daily, HOLD for loose stools	Continue	Discontinue	Modify

Figure 4-3: Medication Reconciliation by Drug Classifications

cation therapies following discharge from the hospital. It also enables the physician to more readily see duplicate drug therapies, as well as opportunities for a combination drug, taking one pill that contains two medications. The addition of dosing parameters for each medication, including maximum dosing, further supports cognitive workflow by reducing the demands on memory of the dosing ranges of these and numerous other medications.

Clinicians expend a significant amount of time and energy scrutinizing patient data and trying to integrate it with their knowledge.[5] Their work is often complicated by poorly structured, ambiguous and sometimes conflicting information from multiple sources.[12] Usability evaluation methods for better supporting clinicians in successfully navigating cognitive workflow in the EHRs, such as cognitive walkthrough and think aloud protocol, can be found in the next chapter.

Context. Human cognition in complex areas such as healthcare is largely context-dependent.[7] EHRs, on the other hand, are often not context-dependent. A simple example about static workflow that does not rely on context follows.[13] This example involves the respiratory assessment in the EHR that includes a series of questions.

Clinician:	*"Mr. Solovy, when you walk down the street, how many blocks can you go before you get winded?"*
Mr. Solovy:	*"I'm a rheumatoid arthritic in the hospital for hip replacement surgery. I don't walk the street."*
Clinician:	*"OK. When you climb the stairs, how many flights can you climb before you get winded?"*
Mr. Solovy:	*"I'm a rheumatoid arthritic in the hospital for hip replacement surgery. I don't climb the stairs."*
Clinician:	*"How do you get around?"*
Mr. Solovy:	*"Cars and elevators."*

As you can see, the assessment is designed to ask every patient the same thing. It is not only insensitive to the context but also increases clinicians' cognitive load and slows productivity as clinicians wade through questions or content that is irrelevant to the patient in front of them. In processing standard content in the EHR, clinicians have to cognitively weed out information not relevant to the situation at hand.

This is what Karsh and colleagues refer to as "one size fits all" fallacy.[14] The authors explain that practice needs differ for different clinical roles in different clinical situations in different clinical environments in different institutions. EHRs are often context-naïve.

For example, a physician inputs an order for "Drug X 7 mg PO daily." In many EHRs, the pharmacist who dispenses the medication and the nurse who administers the medication will see the same data the physician inputs: "Drug X 7 mg PO daily." Good usability, taking into consideration the context of the clinician workflow and how the drug is formulated, would dictate that the pharmacist and the nurse see something to the effect: "Drug X 7 mg (5 mg+2 mg) PO daily."[13]

Cognitive workflow also comes into play in this example of workflow related to context. By delivering the data in the needed form to the pharmacist and nurse, their cognitive workflow is supported and cognitive workload reduced. Potential errors are reduced as they are cued that the medication to be dispensed or administered is two pills, one 5 mg and the other 2 mg. This illustrates how the multiple dimensions of clinical workflow can work synergistically.

Structured forms, often used in EHRs, frequently ignore workflow context. They are easy to design and build and at first glance may give the illusion of supporting cognitive workflow. On the contrary, they create unnecessary and sometimes risky workflows resulting in decreased productivity and user satisfaction. The context of workflow becomes increasingly important with clinical decision support.

Collaboration. Healthcare involves teams of people working together to achieve outcomes. As such, EHRs need to support efficient and effective collaboration in the workflows of multiple healthcare professionals while they perform different roles, often simultaneously, while also striving to achieve common goals for the patient.[15] This quality of collaboration among the healthcare team has a direct impact on both clinical and financial outcomes.

The assessment and treatment of patients represent fundamental workflows in healthcare and are highly collaborative activities.[16] EHR applications are largely designed to mimic paper-based tools, having different places for different clinicians to document these activities.[5] As such, these systems can provide insufficient support for the necessary collaborative workflow.

Similar to assessment and treatment, CPOE is a highly collaborative workflow. While CPOE is typically designed for the tasks of individual providers entering orders, the stage prior to entering the order is highly collaborative, typically involving discussions among clinicians, the patient and family.[17] Similarly, the stage following order entry is also equally collaborative in ensuring the work is done with efficiency and synergy.

It should also be brought out that CPOE involves cognitive workflow and specific contexts. Having ready access to patient data in a meaningful manner supports physicians, advanced practice registered nurses (APRNs) and physician assistants (PAs) as they make decisions for patient treatments. This is another example of how the multiple dimensions of clinical workflow do not exist singularly and in isolation but are combined to create complex workflows.

Collaborative aspects of workflow also cross care settings significantly. These workflows will increase as the focus of healthcare changes from episodic care to the continuum of care. To succeed, EHRs must be designed to facilitate collaboration between clinicians, patients and families across and within varying environments of care.[9] As Karsh states, "This will require more than just putting a new 'front end' on a standard core; it needs to inform the fundamental design of the system."[9]

Electronic tools used to enhance collaborative workflow include threaded discussions or waves, which may include documents, images or pictures. Instant messaging can be used to enhance collaborative workflow. Social media is increasingly being used to enhance collaboration workflows with patients as they become more engaged in their healthcare. Good usability of these collaborative workflow tools will be important for effective collaboration.

Communication. While often viewed as similar to collaboration, communication differs in that it involves the exchange of information, whereas collaboration is about working together, such as in decision making or problem solving. Communication and collaboration are similar in that they both have desired goals, which must be considered in EHR design.

A lot has been written on how EHRs change communication workflows, typically reducing the type and amount of direct interaction, as healthcare professionals access the computer from anywhere to communicate. In so doing, visual cues that were present during the paper-based system are lost. Changes in communication workflow that were not predicted and improved prior to EHR implementation can result in a serious breakdown of communication, creating patient safety risks.[18]

A good example of alteration in communication workflow is a physician remotely logging into his/her computer to review the patient's record and inputting orders into CPOE. How do clinicians charged with carrying out those orders know that the orders have been placed? This is especially pertinent as clinicians are often logged into the computer. In the past, clinicians had a visual cue of the physician making rounds or at least talking with them on the phone. How does the physician communicate with the healthcare team when not physically present?

It is important to appreciate that communication requires both a sender and a receiver. While some refer to one-way communication and two-way communication, both parties must be knowingly engaged for communication to occur. This is especially important when patient care is involved.

Use of one-way electronic communication features in EHRs can fail the test of communication if only the sender side is guaranteed. If one-way communication includes a read-receipt type feature, then receipt can be known. However, the communication of time sensitive information is prohibited, as timely receipt cannot be insured.

An example of good communication workflow within the EHR is the use of electronic whiteboards. Health Insurance Portability and Accountability Act (HIPAA) regulations to protect patient privacy imposed restrictions on the ability to post information such as patient names and medical conditions on large whiteboards—electronic or otherwise—that could potentially be viewed by the public. A smaller version, which often includes additional information desired by clinicians, can be included in the EHR, visible only by clinicians and accessed from anywhere.

The US Department of Veterans Affairs (VA) has been using electronic health records for more than a decade. A recent study at the VA illustrated variations in EHR use resulting in questions about how best to integrate EHRs into clinical workflow.[19] An important finding was how the EHR can facilitate communication workflow for activities such as reporting test results, but can be a barrier when face-to-face communication is required for complex care coordination or urgent care issues.

Communication workflow with patients will be another challenge for EHRs as more patients move into the electronic world of healthcare. Access, computer literacy, language, reading level, health literacy and disabilities will present multiple communication workflow issues to overcome. EHRs and personal health records will open a new world of information for patients. How to effectively communicate healthcare information to and from patients is still largely unknown.

Coordination. Coordination of care is a huge undertaking in healthcare, offering many opportunities for EHRs to support workflows. Clinicians need support in hospitals coordinating care between shifts, between care units before and after transfers, between care units and diagnostic areas, between the cadre of healthcare professionals, between multiple physicians seeing the same patient and between the clinicians, patients and families. Coordination of care between settings is another area of opportunity. Patients also need help in coordinating their own care in order to be in the right place at the right time. Efficiently and effectively coordinating care is significant in reducing delayed access to care or prolonged hospitalizations that place patients at greater risk and incur unnecessary costs.

EHRs are fundamentally databases composed of data gathered by multiple clinicians and medical devices. A study by Reddy and colleagues demonstrated that when clinicians were in the EHR looking for information, it was typically not about their patient but about the work of other clinicians and what actions they had taken with regard to the patient.[20] Clinicians use the EHR to stay informed about what others are doing for the patient, thereby supporting effective workflow coordination.[15]

Current EHRs provide support for what is considered independent workflows such as patient assessment, recognizing they are not patient-specific patient assessments, as mentioned previously. Each clinician does an assessment, documenting it in the designated area in the EHR. There is no coordination in the workflow of patient assessment.

The question is whether patient assessments should be coordinated within the EHR so as to diminish duplicate efforts by different clinicians in diverse areas of the EHR, as well as patients being asked the same questions repeatedly. Good usability would support a more coordinated workflow of clinicians—completing the picture of patient assessment drawing from the unique perspective of each professional discipline. In contrast to the findings of Reddy and colleagues that clinicians use the EHR to view the work of others, this would result in all clinicians viewing the same patient assessment information.

Workflow Exceptions. The work of healthcare is a uniquely complex and a changing combination of routines and exceptions. While there are prescribed orders, plans of care, policies and procedures and other guidelines to support clinical practice, there are also exceptions to all of these that clinicians must deal with daily, and consequently so must EHRs.

An example of exceptions in healthcare workflow involves medication therapy. It is commonly viewed that physicians order medications, pharmacists verify the medication orders and nurses administer the medications, but there are numerous exceptions to this seemingly simple and linear workflow. In emergency situations, nurses administer medications without physician orders or pharmacy verification. There are also times when physicians order medications and pharmacists verify the medication orders, but nurses do not administer because the patient is nauseated or vomiting, the patient refuses the medication, the patient is unavailable as they are in radiology, the medication is contraindicated based on the patient's current vital signs or laboratory findings, and many other reasons. There are also times when physicians, pharmacists or others, such as respiratory therapists or radiology technologists, administer medications. On occasion, nurses can administer medications by protocol or standing delegated orders, but only in those states that allow that exception. And even in those states that allow it, some hospitals will allow it while others will not. There are also medications, such as vaccines (but only the flu and pneumonia vaccines), that are viewed as preventive and do not require a physician order of any type—except sometimes they must be entered as orders for the hospital to be reimbursed.

Similar examples occur in physician offices where workflows are viewed as being simpler. A routine office visit, generally scheduled for 15 minutes, may take longer depending on whether the patient with diabetes, heart failure or chronic lung disease is in good control or not. It may also take longer if subtle cues to more serious problems have not yet been noticed by the patient but are picked up on by the clinician during a routine exam. The wide variations in patients and their conditions that require an equally wide variation in diagnostics and communications with specialists can alter workflows in physician practices fairly quickly and routinely.

Exceptions to workflow are commonplace in healthcare, often providing the greatest challenges in patient care, as well as the greatest potential for errors, making the need for EHR support all the more imperative.[15] In their seminal report on errors in healthcare, the Institute of Medicine encouraged people to "anticipate the unexpected" in order to prevent errors.[21] The same edict should be used in the design of EHRs.

TOWARD A DEFINITION OF CLINICAL WORKFLOW

The lack of a standard definition of clinical workflow in healthcare is problematic as much of the user dissatisfaction is related to workflow. Current EHR architectures are designed for capturing and exchanging patient data, falling short in supporting the workflows of patient care, which underlie the essence of healthcare.[22]

Too often EHRs are forcing standardization in workflows where it does not or should not exist. The underlying belief is that clinical workflows are simple and standardization will make it easier for clinicians to use the EHR. This is not proving to be the case.

A clearer definition of what is meant by clinical workflow is needed. To begin the dialog, one is offered here:

> *Clinical workflow is the multidimensional, transforming processes clinicians use to achieve patient-centered goals.*

Using this definition provides opportunities to advance EHR usability by improving clinical workflow. In lieu of simplistic, linear views of workflow, which are appealing because they are easier to comprehend and implement, it is important to take an in-depth holistic view of clinical practices. This provides us with a greater appreciation of the complexities of clinical workflow and prevents the loss of important and necessary information about professional practice in healthcare.

The design of EHRs at one extreme requires users to adapt their workflow to the application.[15] At the other extreme is the EHR designed to accommodate the workflow of clinicians.[15] In either case, or somewhere between the two extremes, an accurate definition of clinical workflow is required. Equally important is a definition that is understood by both clinicians and designers, enabling them to work together to achieve the best EHRs.

CONCLUSION

Whether implementing a new EHR, optimizing a current EHR, or changing to a different EHR system, getting clinical workflow right is not for the faint of heart. The nonlinear, fast-paced, multitasking, rapidly changing, frequently interrupted work of healthcare professionals makes supporting workflow both incredibly important and significantly challenging. It is imperative to consider not only the physical aspects of workflow but also the cognitive, contextual, collaborative, communication, and coordination aspects, as well as the exceptions. Several of the usability evaluation techniques outlined in the next chapter will aid in better understanding clinical workflows. The important point to remember is that approaching workflow using only one approach will fall short due to the multidimensional nature of clinical workflow. The next chapter, Chapter 5, describes several of the usability evaluation methods that will help move this effort forward in achieving the goal of EHRs with excellent usability.

REFERENCES

1. Ribitzky R, Sterling MA, Bradley V. EHR usability pain points survey Q4 2009. Presented at the 2010 Annual HIMSS Conference & Exhibition, March 1-4, 2010; Atlanta, GA.

2. Unertl KM, Novak LL, Johnson KB, et al. Traversing the many paths of workflow research: Developing a conceptual framework of workflow terminology through a systematic literature review. *J Am Med Inform Assoc.* 2010; 17:265-73.

3. Carayon P, Karsh BT, Cartmill RS, et al. *Incorporating Health Information Technology Into Workflow Redesign – Summary Report.* (Prepared by the Center for Quality and Productivity Improvement, University of Wisconsin–Madison, under Contract No. HHSA 290-2008-10036C). AHRQ Publication No. 10-0098-EF. Rockville, MD: Agency for Healthcare Research and Quality. October 2010.

4. Cain C, Haque S. Organizational workflow and its impact on work and quality. In: Hughes RG, ed. *Patient Safety and Quality: An Evidence-Based Handbook for Nurses.* AHRQ Publication No. 08-0043. Rockville, MD: Agency for Healthcare Research and Quality. April 2008.

5. National Research Council. *Computational Technology for Effective Health Care: Immediate Steps and Strategic Direction.* Washington, DC: National Academies Press, 2009.

6. Kirsh D. Adaptive rooms, virtual collaboration, and cognitive workflow. Proceedings of the First International Workshop on Cooperative Buildings, Integrating Information, Organization, and Architecture. 1998; 94-106.

7. Horsky J, Zhang J, Patel VL. To err is not entirely human: complex technology and user cognition. *J Biomed Inform.* 2005; 38:264e6.

8. Karsh BT, Holden RJ, Alper SJ, et al. A human factors engineering paradigm for patient safety: Designing to support the performance of the healthcare professional. *Quality & Safety in Health Care.* 2006; 15 Suppl 1:i59-65.

9. Karsh BT. Clinical practice improvement and redesign: how change in workflow can be supported by clinical decision support. AHRQ Publication No. 09-0054-EF. Rockville, Maryland: Agency for Healthcare Research and Quality. June 2009.

10. Weir CR, Nebeker JJR, Hicker BL, et al. A cognitive task analysis of information management strategies in a computerized order entry environment. *J Am Med Inform Assoc.* 2007; 14(1):65-75.

11. Woods DD. Designs are hypotheses about how artifacts shape cognition and collaboration. *Ergonomics.* 1998; 41:168-173.

12. Kushniruk AW. Analysis of complex decision-making processes in health care: Cognitive approaches to health informatics. *J Biomed Inform.* 2001; 34:365-376.

13. Solovy A. Static workflow. *Hosp Health Netw.* 2006 May; 30.

14. Karsh BT, Weinger MB, Abbott PA, et al. Health information technology: Fallacies and sober realities. *J Am Med Inform Assoc.* 2010; 17:617-623.

15. Pratt W, Reddy MC, McDonald DW, et al. Incorporating ideas from computer-supported cooperative work. *J Biomed Inform.* 2004; 37(2):128-137.

16. Horsky J, Zhang J, Patel VL. To err is not entirely human: complex technology and user cognition. *J Biomed Inform.* 2005; 38:264e6.

17. Aarts J, Ash J, Berg M. Extending the understanding of computerized physician order entry: Implications for professional collaboration, workflow and quality of care. *Int J Med Inform.* 2006; 76(Suppl):S4-S13.

18. Institute of Medicine. *Health IT and Patient Safety: Building Safer Systems for Better Care.* Washington, DC: The National Academies Press, 2012.

19. Saleem JJ, Flanagan ME, Russ AL, et al. You and me and the computer makes three: Variations in exam room use of the electronic health record. *J American Med Inform Assoc.* 2013; 0:1-5.

20. Reddy M, Dourish P, Pratt W. Coordinating Heterogeneous Work: Information and Representation in Medical Care. In: European Conference on Computer Supported Cooperative Work (ECSCW'01), Bonn, Germany. 2001; 39-258.

21. Institute of Medicine. *To Err is Human - Building a Safer Health System.* Washington, DC: The National Academies Press, 2000.

22. Kuziemsky CE, Williams JB, Weber-Jahnke JH. Towards electronic health record support for collaborative processes. In: *Proceedings of the 3rd Workshop on Software Engineering in Health Care.* New York, NY: ACM. 2001; 32-39.

CHAPTER 5

Usability Evalution Methods

"We shall neither fail nor falter; we shall not weaken or tire...
Give us the tools and we will finish the job."
—Winston Churchill, February 9, 1941

It is time to put some tools in your toolbox. This chapter describes several methods that can be used to evaluate and improve the usability of an EHR. The intention is to provide for you an overview of each method, so you can decide which of the methods would best fit with the usability work you are doing. In most cases, the information is sufficient to enable the reader to conduct EHR usability evaluations.

This chapter is organized from simple methods like affinity diagramming to the penultimate method called TURF, each offering a different view of your EHR usability. As you will learn, TURF is a comprehensive framework that encompasses multiple evaluation methods. We have discussed in the preceding chapters the importance of evaluating EHR usability from different angles, similar to taking a full set of vital signs and not just the heart rate. Heart rate alone is insufficient information to appreciate the impact of the EHR usability under evaluation.

For each method in the chapter, there is a short description of the advantages and an explanation of how the method is conducted, along with a list of possible variations on the basic method. There is also an example (or key aspects of an example where a complete description is impractical) and a list of pros and cons associated with the use of the method. Finally, there is a brief summary of each method.

SIMPLE USABILITY EVALUATION METHODS

Affinity Diagramming
Description. Affinity diagrams are useful for rapidly uncovering information on usability when insufficient information is known. They are a low-technology, quick and collaborative technique for organizing a plethora of ideas into categories. This method is attributed to Jiro Kawakita, a Japanese archaeologist who formalized affinity diagrams in the 1960s.[1,2] The technique is simple to implement and can be used whenever the

goal is to quickly collect ideas, as in brainstorming, and then look for common themes; or when there are many complex issues that must be distilled to a manageable number.

Using Affinity Diagramming

Participants: Requires a facilitator and participants. The more participants there are, the more ideas that will be collected (recognizing that participants must be able to fit into the meeting room or work space).

Materials: Sticky notes or cards, markers, large surface where all notes can be viewed by participants, sheets of ten colored stickers for each participant

Process:

1. Facilitator clearly describes the activity to participants including the purpose (which is to gather a lot of ideas on the topic of interest) and how the participants will be involved.
2. Without speaking, participants individually record each idea or reaction to the guiding question on a separate sticky note or card.
3. Participants are then instructed to silently place all cards without constraints where they can be viewed by all participants (Figure 5-1). This could be a wall, a table or even the floor.
4. Once all ideas have been gathered, participants are asked to place the cards that are similar near each other without speaking (Figure 5-2).
   a. Cards can be moved more than once by participants if they change their minds about where a particular card belongs in relation to the other cards.
   b. Cards can be duplicated if participants initially think they should belong to more than one group.
   c. Ask people to be mindful to how they are arranging the cards.
5. Once the cards have been arranged in groups, the facilitator picks a card that is most representative of the group of cards or creates a new card to use as the label for each group of cards.
6. The facilitator then asks the participants to validate that the group heading is accurate and makes adjustment as needed based on group consensus.

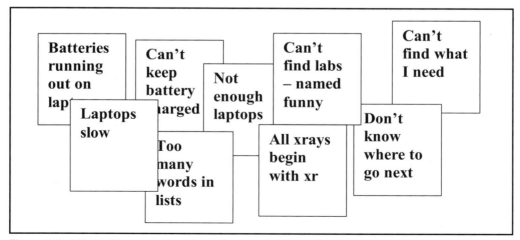

Figure 5-1: Affinity Diagramming: Ideas Captured Without Constraints

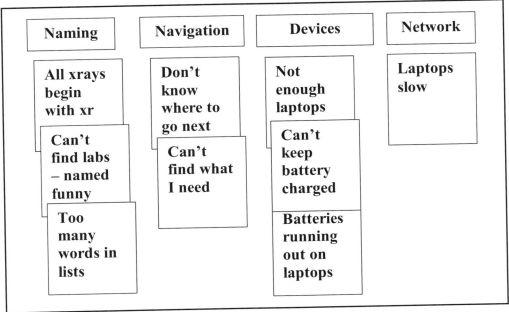

Figure 5-2: Affinity Diagramming: Ideas Arranged into Topics[3]

7. Cards are then prioritized by asking participants to, while maintaining silence, use their stickers to cast votes for the most important cards. A participant can use any number of their stickers on a single card if he or she chooses.
8. Debrief with participants and document the outcome.
9. Use the findings to identify further evaluation needed or to create action plans.

Variations:
- Have each participant take several minutes to describe the reasoning behind their choices.
- Use different colored topic cards.
- Arrange the cards in ways that screens or menus would be laid out.
- Engage diverse stakeholders to ensure diverse ideas.

Summary. Figure 5-3 outlines the advantages and disadvantages of affinity diagramming. The usability evaluation method is useful for identifying issues and categorizing the similarities so as to create more comprehensive approaches to intervening. Since affinity diagrams can be created with minimal expertise, they can be developed using diverse stakeholders as participants, resulting in an expansive list of ideas or suggestions with fresh perspectives. Affinity diagrams can be created quickly, participants can be energized by their participation, and they can provide insights into how diverse groups of people view the target problem or task. Creating multiple affinity diagrams using different participants can be predicted to create unique views of the problem or issue.

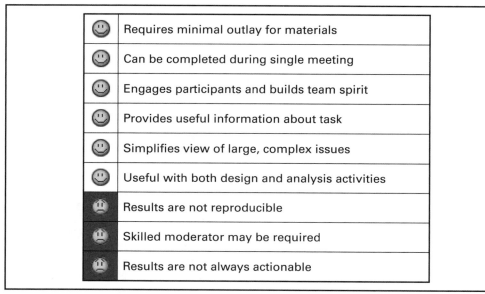

☺	Requires minimal outlay for materials
☺	Can be completed during single meeting
☺	Engages participants and builds team spirit
☺	Provides useful information about task
☺	Simplifies view of large, complex issues
☺	Useful with both design and analysis activities
☹	Results are not reproducible
☹	Skilled moderator may be required
☹	Results are not always actionable

Figure 5-3: Pros and Cons of Affinity Diagramming

Brainstorming

Description. Brainstorming is similar to affinity diagramming for quickly uncovering information about EHR usability when little is known. It is a popular technique for generating ideas and developing solutions to problems. The technique can be used by individuals, but there is much more enthusiasm and better results with group brainstorming. The key concept behind brainstorming is to have participants generate as many ideas as possible by encouraging any and all ideas while minimizing social and personal inhibitors.

Conducting a Brainstorming Session[4,5]

Participants: Facilitator plus three to ten participants

Materials: Wall-based marking board or paper, markers, pen and paper for participants

Process:

1. Facilitator introduces and describes the goal(s) for the brainstorming session.
2. Facilitator leads a short icebreaker whereby participants introduce themselves, such as name, job, or favorite entertainer, which helps to reduce personal inhibitions, allowing for the free flow of ideas.
3. Facilitator states the rules and goals of the brainstorming session.
   a. Topic of brainstorming activity
   b. Amount of time
   c. No side discussions or verbose explanations
   d. No disparaging or other comments that are judgmental
   e. Focus on positives—stating what not to do does not count as an idea
4. Facilitator writes down all ideas and makes them visible to participants (Figure 5-4).
5. Facilitator periodically reminds participants of remaining time.
6. Facilitator saves five minutes at end of period to collect feedback on the process.

7. Analyze findings to determine next steps or create action plans.

Variations:

- Number the ideas so they are easier to reference.
- Create a goal for the number of ideas to be generated. Choose a "stretch goal" that will be hard to achieve, as this tends to create better outcomes.

Summary. Brainstorming is a great usability evaluation method for generating ideas or problem solving,

---

Brainstorming Ideas

- Use a font that is easier to read.
- Put allergies on header.
- Don't use . . .
- Don't use synonyms.
- Place code status on header.
- Don't use words no one knows.
- Don't use icons no one knows.
- Don't use icons that look alike.
- Use red to highlight allergies and code

Figure 5-4: Post Ideas Where They Are Readily Visible[6]

---

but it is important to provide structure to maximize the positive value. The pros and cons to brainstorming are outlined in Figure 5-5. An effective facilitator can determine whether a brainstorming session is effective or disruptive and intervene appropriately. While brainstorming is seen as useful in generating ideas or solutions to usability issues, some argue that brainstorming design issues fail to lead to the best solutions.[7]

Card Sorting

Description. Card sorting is an infrequently used technique that can provide a wealth of information to users about usability issues and solutions.[8] It is especially useful for designing workflows, screen navigations and menu structures.

The basic process of card sorting involves sorting of prelabeled index cards into categories of their own choosing. This is also referred to as an "open" card sort. Variations of this basic process have been created, for example, to have participants sort the cards into predetermined categories. This is known as a "closed" card sort.

Card sorting requires little expense and is quite versatile. Users can validate navigation schemes or how to order choices; card sorts can generate qualitative and quantita-

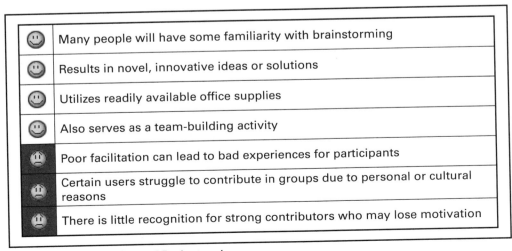

Figure 5-5: Pros and Cons of Brainstorming

tive information, which can prove to be compelling in research or business cases. Not surprisingly, there are a number of software programs available that offer card sorting and analysis capabilities.

Conducting a Card Sort[5,8-10]

Participants: 15 participants provide statistically meaningful information.[11]

Materials: Prelabeled 3"x5" index cards, markers, a surface that is large enough to sort the cards

Process:

1. Facilitator(s) identifies the topic and creates the cards to be sorted. An example might be potential words or terms to be used in a drop-down menu in the EHR. If you are using a large number of cards, consider using mail merge and sheets of printable envelope labels to prepare the card labels.
2. Select the users, and schedule a meeting room that will hold the participants and has enough workspace to spread out the cards.
   a. Estimated time to perform the card sort:
      i. Up to 30 cards: 20 minutes
      ii. 31–50 cards: 30 minutes
      iii. 51–100 cards: 60 minutes
3. Prepare instructions for participants.
4. For inexperienced facilitators, a pilot test can provide excellent preparation.
5. For the actual exercise…
   a. Welcome the participants
   b. Go over the instructions
   c. Perform a simple card sort warm-up (three to five minutes)
   d. Perform the card sort (Figure 5-6).
      i. Have each participant place similar cards together.
      ii. If a card belongs in two or more groups, create a duplicate card with the card contents and place a card in each group.
      iii. For open card sorts, have the participant label the groups after all the cards have been sorted.
   e. Wrap-up—thank participants, explain what happens and whether they will receive any incentives or follow-up information.
6. Tabulate the results (Figure 5-7). The simplest approach is to create a grid with the contents of each card listed in the left-most column and the category name that it is placed in along the top. For open card sorts, do not combine similar concepts or misspellings, as these can be useful to designers.

Variations:
- If a scanner is available, printing bar codes on the cards can be a huge time-saver when it comes to collecting and documenting the cards.
- Use software to perform remote card sorts, enabling Internet-based users to participate. Some programs that are currently available over the Internet include OptimalSort, SimpleCardSort, UsabiliTest, WebSort, ConceptCodify, UserZoom, and CardZort. (These are all commercial services.)

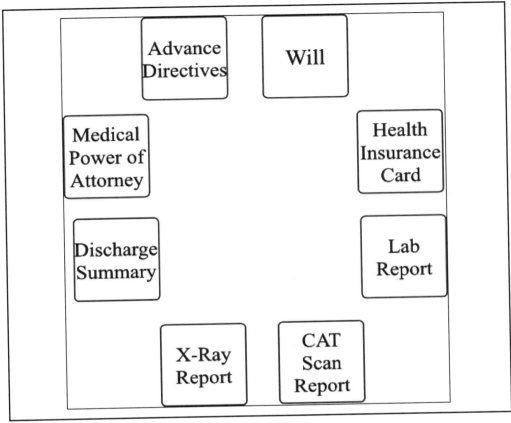

Figure 5-6: Unsorted Cards

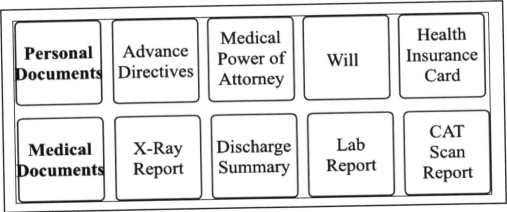

Figure 5-7: Sorted and Categorized Cards from Card Sorting

- For large groups, especially when remote card sorting is used, more complex analysis can be performed. Many of the software programs listed previously will provide these capabilities.
- In a reverse card sort, participants are given cards that are previously sorted into categories and they are asked how they would find a function or perform a

😊	User centered
😊	Simple, easy to understand
😊	Low cost
😊	Can be scaled to large number of participants
😊	All stakeholders can be engaged
😊	Quantitative data available
🙁	Results can vary dramatically
🙁	Advanced analysis can be time consuming if done manually
🙁	Most online tools are fee based

Figure 5-8: Pros and Cons of Card Sorting

task with the organization they are given. This can be used to validate an existing menu structure or look for areas of confusion.

Summary. Card sorting is a usability evaluation method that should be in every toolbox. The pros and cons of the method are outlined in Figure 5-8. It is typically low cost, can be done quickly, provides qualitative and quantitative information and can be used to involve all stakeholders on a project. Card sorting is used to evaluate the navigation structure, order information presented to the user and validate content. With access to online tools, card sorting techniques can be utilized by large numbers of participants, enabling advanced statistical analyses.

Checklists

Description. Checklists are best thought of as a class of tool as opposed to a specific usability evaluation method. Checklists exist to organize thoughts and activities and are often used in group settings to ensure that participants are aware of steps to follow or to guide their actions. As live demonstrations of the utility of external representation, checklists greatly reduce the burden of remembering information. Because of the ubiquitous nature of checklists, you will find more examples in lieu of "how to" information.

Examples. The following checklist was developed by Deniese Pierotti of Xerox Corporation in the early 1990s (Figure 5-9). The checklist is not shown in its entirety; however, the full checklist can be found at http://www.stcsig.org/usability/topics/articles/he-checklist.html.[12] There are links to other checklists following this checklist.

Heuristic Evaluation—A System Checklist

1. Visibility of System Status

The system should always keep the user informed about what is going on through appropriate feedback within a reasonable time.

#	Review Checklist	Yes	No	N/A	Comments
1.1	Does every display begin with a title or header that describes screen contents?	❑	❑	❑	
1.2	Is there a consistent icon design scheme and stylistic treatment across the system?	❑	❑	❑	
1.3	Is a single, selected icon clearly visible when surrounded by unselected icons?	❑	❑	❑	
1.4	Do menu instructions, prompts, and error messages appear in the same place(s) on each menu?	❑	❑	❑	
1.5	In multipage data entry screens, is each page labeled to show its relation to others?	❑	❑	❑	
1.6	If overtype and insert mode are both available, is there a visible indication of which one the user is in?	❑	❑	❑	
1.7	If pop-up windows are used to display error messages, do they allow the user to see the field in error?	❑	❑	❑	
1.8	Is there some form of system feedback for every operator action?	❑	❑	❑	
1.9	After the user completes an action (or group of actions), does the feedback indicate that the next group of actions can be started?	❑	❑	❑	
1.10	Is there visual feedback in menus or dialog boxes about which choices are selectable?	❑	❑	❑	
1.11	Is there visual feedback in menus or dialog boxes about which choice the cursor is on now?	❑	❑	❑	
1.12	If multiple options can be selected in a menu or dialog box, is there visual feedback about which options are already selected?	❑	❑	❑	
1.13	Is there visual feedback when objects are selected or moved?	❑	❑	❑	
1.14	Is the current status of an icon clearly indicated?	❑	❑	❑	

Figure 5-9: Usability Evaluation Checklist

Below are some useful checklists, including some that are lists of checklists.
- Catch common usability problems: http://userium.com/
- 25-point website usability checklist: http://tinyurl.com/ack77s
- 45 web design checklists and questionnaires: http://tinyurl.com/mo48uu
- 25 useful usability cheat sheets and checklists: http://tinyurl.com/pwbmwm

Summary. The pros and cons of using checklists in usability evaluation are outlined in Figure 5-10. Checklists are valuable memory aids that ensure users do not overlook or forget key points or aspects of a process or activity. They also serve as easy-to-construct tools to make processes repeatable by delineating the key characteristics or steps that users should follow. Since checklists can be implemented electronically, they can also be used as a tracking tool or to identify troubling activities.

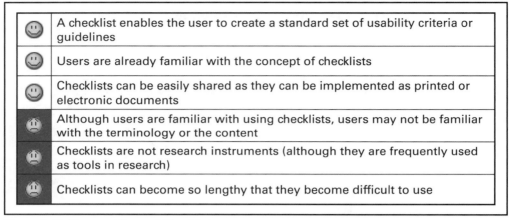

😊	A checklist enables the user to create a standard set of usability criteria or guidelines
😊	Users are already familiar with the concept of checklists
😊	Checklists can be easily shared as they can be implemented as printed or electronic documents
☹	Although users are familiar with using checklists, users may not be familiar with the terminology or the content
☹	Checklists are not research instruments (although they are frequently used as tools in research)
☹	Checklists can become so lengthy that they become difficult to use

Figure 5-10: Pros and Cons of Checklists

MODERATELY DIFFICULT USABILITY EVALUATION METHODS

Clinical Workflow Analysis

Description. Clinical workflow analysis describes the process of identifying existing clinical workflows along with the involved actors in the workflows, abstracting and decomposing these workflows to identify how they provide value to users or how they allow for unwanted consequences. Based on the analysis, alternative clinical workflows can be developed that streamline the workflow, reduce negative consequences and improve the quality of care.

Clinical workflow analysis demands qualitative and quantitative skills from the informaticists.[13] Processes can include formal steps, as well as activities derived from experientially acquired knowledge. Thoroughly understanding existing workflows is vital to the implementation of EHRs, and failures to successfully implement usable workflows are cited as sources of unintended adverse consequences (UACs).[14]

Conducting Clinical Workflow Analysis

Participants: The scope of clinical workflow analysis can vary dramatically, and the personnel required will tend to mirror the complexity of the workflow being examined. For a workflow that addresses a limited, targeted procedure, such as taking vital signs in the exam room of a solitary practitioner, the following skills are recommended:

- Observer experienced in ethnographic (or *in situ*) observations
- Workflow analyst with domain knowledge and experience translating observation information into workflow components

Materials:

- Description of observation guidelines
- Tools for recording workflow activities
  - Video recorder
  - Audio recorder
  - Diagram of the worksite with codes for key personnel, locations and objects
  - Log (paper or electronic)

- Markers
- Clock
- Tools for diagramming workflows (e.g., Bonita Open Solution, Microsoft Visio, Dia Diagram Editor, ARIS)

Process:
1. Administrative preparation:
   a. Determine if institutional review board (IRB) approval is required.
   b. Where appropriate, solicit permission of patients to observe processes.
2. Information gathering:
   a. Determine whether shadowing key personnel or observing key location will provide richest information.
   b. Position recording devices where they will have the best likelihood of capturing relevant activities.
      i. Recording devices are very useful because activities can occur rapidly and involve multiple participants and objects.
   c. Start recording devices.
   d. Using codes for personnel, locations and objects, log who does what activity at which location using which resources at what time and for how long.
      i. It is important that the observer remains as unobtrusive as possible throughout the observation period.
      ii. The observer should not make suggestions or comments.
3. Analysis:
   a. Using the activity log and the recording devices, identify the personnel and resources that are required for the workflow to proceed.
   b. Similarly, identify how the workflow is impeded or disrupted by missing or misplaced people or objects.
   c. Determine optimum process times by measuring how long the process takes from beginning to end if there are no unnecessary delays or wait periods.
   d. Compare the optimum times against the actual times to identify opportunities for improving process times.
   e. Identify where mistakes or errors occur and identify the contributing factors.
      i. Look for resources that are misplaced, misused or missing.
      ii. Other factors include fatigue, competing activities (such as meals or breaks, interruptions by peers, documentation duties, emergencies, time-sensitive tasks) or environmental distractions (noisy environment, poor lighting, uncomfortable temperatures, etc.).
4. Feedback:
   a. After compiling the workflow, review the findings with the stakeholders to ensure there is agreement that the analysis fits their perception of the workflow.
   b. Make any corrections and conduct a final review.

Variations:
- Utilize hardware devices like radio frequency ID chips (RFID) to track user movements.[13,15] These can also be attached to objects that can be moved.

- Make multiple observations of the workflow, focusing on different aspects of the workflow (such as what information is exchanged) or shadowing a different person.
- Model the workflow with simulation software to visualize the as-is and to-be states.[16]
- Collaborate with other professionals who are trying to understand their clinical workflows.[17]

Examples. The following examples are from a workbook document developed by Masspro, the Medicare Quality Improvement Organization for Massachusetts (Figures 5-11 to 5-13).[18] The document contains numerous forms and examples that can be used

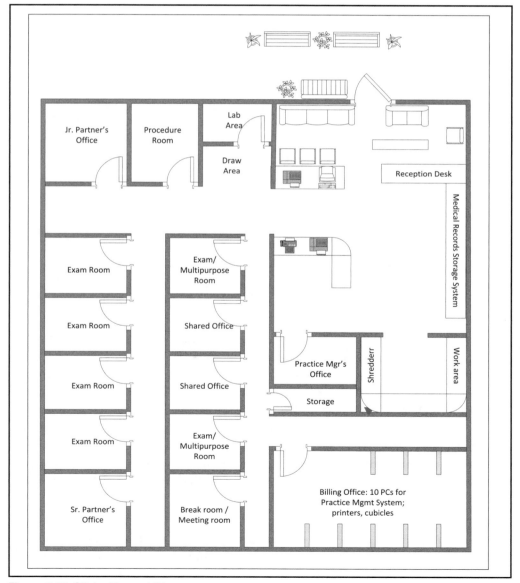

Figure 5-11: Clinical Layout Diagram

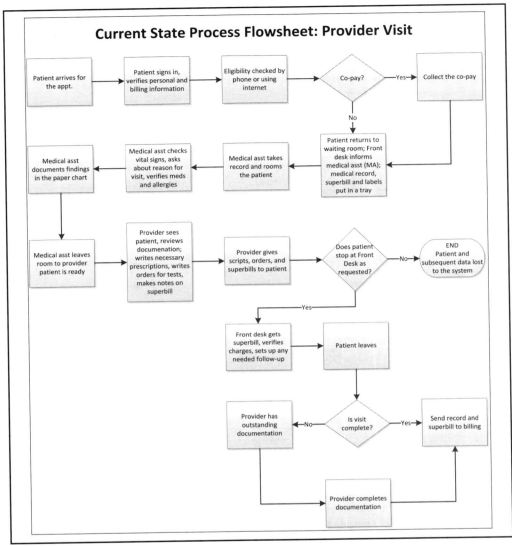

Figure 5-12: Current State Flowsheet

to kickstart the workflow analysis process. The practice in the following examples and any references to people or events are fictitious.

Summary. Clinical workflow analysis is arguably one of the most important tools but should not be used alone, as doing so will present an incomplete picture. Healthcare is literally defined by workflow as patients encounter a variety of professionals and administrators as they travel through the healthcare system. Physicians, nurses and other healthcare professionals rely on knowing what duties each other performs, as well as how materials, like beds and supplies, are allocated. During emergencies, well-coordinated workflows can have a profound effect on the effectiveness of the healthcare team.[19]

Clinical workflow analysis becomes even more vital as organizations are implementing new EHRs or replacing existing EHRs.[20,21] The consequences of poorly implemented workflows, such as lost productivity, increased time to complete processes,

Check-In
What type of information is gathered by the front desk at check-in? ■ Verification of name and address   ■ Verification of insurance ■ Copy of insurance card   ❑ HIPAA forms ❑ Other:
If you are using a Property Management System (PMS), what information must be entered or checked at each visit? *Address, insurance information*
List any information that goes forward with the chart after check-in. ■ Superbill   ❑ Extra labels   ■ Patient Hx/ROS Forms ❑ Other:
Do you collect co-pays at check-in?   ■ Yes   ❑ No
How does the clinical staff know the patient has arrived? *Chart is in the rack* *If waiting room gets too backed up, front desk staff gets the medical assistant (MA)*
Rooming the Patient
Who takes the patient to the exam room?   ■ MA   ❑ MD   ❑ Nurse Other:
Is the chart reviewed for outstanding tasks by the rooming staff?   ■ Yes   ❑ No How is this information communicated to the provider for action? *Medical asst places green sticky note on the outside of the chart*
What information is gathered before the provider sees the patient? ■ Reason for visit   ■ Vital signs   ■ Meds reviewed ■ Allergies reviewed Other:
Are any tests done before the provider sees the patient?   ■ Yes   ❑ No If yes, please list: *Depends on patient's problem list*
Is the information gathered written on a specific type of form?   ❑ Yes   ❑ No
If yes, is the form specific to a type of visit?   ❑ Yes   ❑ No
How does the provider know that the patient is ready to be seen? Describe: *"Ready" light is turned on*

Figure 5-13: Analysis of Provider Visit (page 1 of 2)

Provider Seeing the Patient
What information does the provider review prior to entering the exam room?
Where is this information located/accessed? *All information is in the chart*
Where are the medications and diagnoses lists maintained? *The inside left side of the jacket has current lists for both*
What forms (if any) are used during a visit? *"Encounter" form and "New orders" form*
Where are the charges/diagnoses captured for the visit? *These are part of the "Encounter"*
Are patient education handouts given during the provider visits? ❏ Yes ❏ No
Who delivers services like the immunizations, ear irrigations, etc.? ■ Provider   ■ Medical asst.   ■ Nurse   ■ Other:
If not the provider, how does the person know that the patient needs these services and is ready for them? Describe: *Orders are detailed on the inside left page of the record and the "Ready" light shows readiness.*
If the patient requires specific follow-up (appointments, referral, lab, etc.), how are these communicated by the provider? *The encounter form lists these and then they are posted to the medical record.*
Check-Out
Do you collect co-pays at checkout? ❏ Yes   ❏ No
What information does the patient bring back to the front desk? *Encounter form and medical record*

How do you handle future appointments?
   ❏ Have patient complete a postcard that is then filed and sent later as a reminder
   ❏ Make a future appointment but only if less than 6 months into the future
Other:

Do you schedule appointments for tests or referrals to other providers? ❏ Yes ❏ No If yes, how do you do this?
What happens to charges for the day's visit? *Sent to billing staff for submission and coding*

Figure 5-13: Analysis of Provider Visit (page 2 of 2)

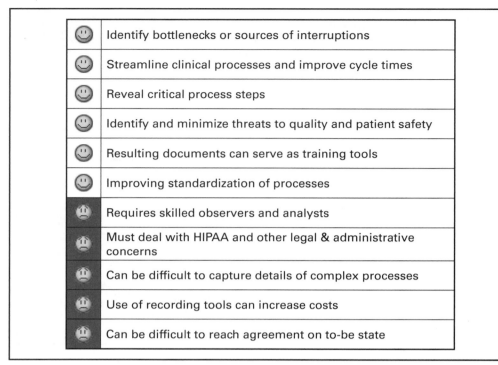

Figure 5-14: Pros and Cons of Clinical Workflow Analysis

processes that do not match the way work needs to be done, are frequently cited as sources of dissatisfaction around EHRs and represent risks to safety and patient care.[22-25] Pros and cons to clinical workflow analysis are presented in Figure 5-14.

Cognitive Walkthrough

Description. A cognitive walkthrough is a type of usability inspection that has participants perform predefined tasks with the application while noting issues that they encounter during this process. Cognitive walkthroughs were designed to explore how readily a user could "walk up and use" an application, with the underlying premise that applications that require extensive manuals and formal training are creating barriers to usability.[5,26]

Cognitive walkthroughs offer two big enticements. On one hand, cognitive walkthroughs are an economical, practical method that can be implemented without real-world users during any stage of development in which the user interface is being modeled or implemented. In addition to the business benefits, cognitive walkthroughs are a valuable source of feedback to designers about how well their concept of the way users will work matches the way the user expects the application to work.

There are four questions that should be addressed during a successful cognitive walkthrough[27,28]:

1. Will the user try to achieve the correct effect?
2. Will the user notice that the correct action is available?
3. Will the user associate the correct action with the desired effect?
4. Will the user notice that progress is being made toward the desired goal?

Participants: Cognitive walkthroughs can be performed with a single user or with small groups.[29]

Materials:

- A description of the tasks or function that the participant is to perform
- Mockups of the interface or a working interface
- Forms (preferred) for documenting the walkthrough process

Process:

1. Preparation:
   a. Identify the key tasks that are to be covered during the cognitive walkthrough. Focus on tasks that are likely to be used frequently or in critical situations, such as entering vital signs or responding to drug-drug interaction alerts.
   b. Develop guidance for the participants so they will understand the types of items that you want them to be alert to and to keep track of. Some users may be reluctant to identify problems, as they may be inclined to blame any frustrations on themselves.
   c. Users may find it helpful to have a worksheet or template to use for noting issues.
2. Limit interactions with the participants unless the participant is unable to make progress or if the participant has stopped annotating his or her experience.
3. If participants are inexperienced, an informaticist can be used to provide live guidance, including prompting when it is observed that the participant is not cognizant of notable behaviors.
4. Provide the participants with a description of the task to be completed. Encourage participants to think of their activities in the context of the goal they are trying to achieve.
   a. What is the goal they are trying to accomplish?
   b. How are the actions they are taking with the system helping to advance toward their goal?
   c. How does the system respond to their actions?
   d. What sources of frustration or errors do they encounter?[30]
5. Review the findings with the designers to identify issues that have been raised. Consider classifying the items based on the impact to users first, along with the time required to make changes.

Variations:

- Utilize experienced usability personnel to perform the walkthrough.
- Use audio and video equipment to record participant behaviors and comments. This provides the ability to review periods during which the participant is moving rapidly or is less verbal.
- Have the participants complete a usability survey after the cognitive walkthrough in order to elicit additional feedback.

Example. Enter the patient's blood pressure (a representative portion of this task is detailed in Figure 5-15).

Goal	User Actions	System Responses	Advancing to Goal?	Issues
Enter blood pressure of 160/120	User moving the mouse while searching for the application's icon.	The system highlights the icon under the mouse but provides no additional information.	No	Application has multiple icons and the complete name is not always visible.
	User clicks on icons to see full application name.	System displays full application name with single click on icon.	Yes	
	User locates desired icon and double-clicks on it.	System loads application. Initial display occurs within 5 seconds; complete application load takes 45 seconds.	Yes	
	User visually scans the application screen to locate cues to Vital Signs.	N/A	No	Vital Signs tab was difficult to locate, as the tabs are not arranged in an apparent order.
	User moves mouse to option on screen for Vital Signs.	Mouse pointer is positioned over Vital Signs tab.	Yes	
	User clicks on Vital Signs hotspot.	System paints the screen with the Vital Signs screen.	Yes	
	User moves mouse while searching for Blood Pressure entry field.	The mouse pointer tracks the movement of the mouse across the screen.	Yes	
	User clicks on "New Vitals" button.	The system mouse pointer changes shape to show that something is happening and after 4 seconds, a "Select Encounter" dialog box is displayed.	Yes	
	The user moves the mouse to the "New Visit" tab.	The mouse pointer tracks the movement of the mouse across the screen.	No	
	The user clicks on "New Visit."	The dialog box shows a text entry field that requires the user to choose a location. The date of the visit is also displayed, along with a checkbox and explanation to mark this as a "Historical Visit."	No	It was unclear how to choose the location. There were tabs for Clinic, Hospital, and New Visit.
	The user clicks on the option "GENERAL RADIOLOGY."	The system populates the "Visit Locations" text box with "GENERAL RADIOLOGY."	No	The location field looks like it is designed for typing in an entry, but clicking on an item in the list populates the field.
	The user clicks on "Select."	The system closes the dialog box and displays the Vital Signs dialog box.	Yes	
	The user locates the field to enter the blood pressure.	N/A	No	
	The user moves the mouse to the field in order to enter the blood pressure.	The mouse pointer tracks the movement of the mouse across the screen. Once over the field, the system provides a tool tip showing how the blood pressure can be entered.	No	Several of the Vital Sign fields are not visible, and it is not obvious that the user must scroll to see them.
	The user clicks in the text box to enable entering text.	The text pointer is displayed on the left side of the text box.	No	
	The user types in the blood pressure as "160/120."	The system displays the characters as they are typed by the user.	Yes	Allowing unstructured text will reduce the ability to analyze data.

Figure 5-15: Cognitive Walkthrough

After completing the walkthrough, the participants are asked to describe any frustrations they encountered during the walkthrough.

☺	"Four Questions" (previously listed) are commonly used standards for guiding evaluators
☺	Identifies errors in designs that will affect user performance
☺	Tends to find serious problems
☺	Useful for modeling walk-up-and-use users (i.e., no training and no manuals)
☺	Can be utilized during early stages of interface development
☹	Planning is important to useful results; key scenarios must be defined
☹	Finds fewer problems than heuristic evaluation
☹	Naïve users may require training on "Four Questions"
☹	List negative points with frowning face

Figure 5-16: Pros and Cons of Cognitive Walkthrough

Summary. Cognitive walkthroughs are attractive because they can be used throughout the development cycle, and they find existing usability issues. They are more likely to identify severe errors, but this can be partially mitigated by preparing and coaching the participants through the process and through the use of instruments to familiarize the participants with what they should to be looking for.[27] Cognitive walkthroughs are most helpful at identifying issues that result from the differences in the way the designers anticipate how users will interact with the system from the way that users actually do interact with the system.

GOMS—Goals, Operators, Methods and Selection Rules

Description. GOMS is an acronym for goals, operators, methods, and selection rules, which refers to the key concepts in this structured cognitive approach to evaluating usability.

- A *goal* is the task to be performed, such as "Beginning at the primary application screen, enter a blood pressure of 160/120." A goal can be broken into subgoals for complex goals.
- *Operators* are the individual activities that the user must execute in order to reach the goal.
- *Methods* are procedures composed of multiple operators.
- *Selection rules* describe the logic to be applied when the user has multiple paths of operators that will all reach the goal. The selection rules determine which path to follow.[29]

GOMS allows us to predict the number of actions and the length of time it will take an expert user to reach the goal. To calculate the predicted time to reach a goal or perform a method, the following guidelines were developed based on timing of actual users. To be clear, GOMS is not intended to model the behavior of new or inexperienced users; the times given here are the amounts of time an average user would expend for specific behaviors.[31]

- 203 ms – Eye fixation
- 30 ms – Eye movement
- 100 ms – Perceptual processing
- 70 ms – Cognitive processing
- 70 ms – Motor processing

Once the procedure is broken into operators, the time to perform each can be estimated by determining which category best describes each operator and then adding up the times for all operators.

Conducting a GOMS Evaluation

How many: One participant

Materials:

- Pencil and paper (or electronic equivalent)
- List of the time estimates

Process:

1. Identify a task that will serve as the GOMS goal. In this case, we will use the task of entering the patient's blood pressure of 160/120.
2. From the initial screen in the application, break down the steps that the user must go through in order to reach the goal state.
   a. Be attentive to:
      i. Situations in which the user must locate cues or links on the screen for the next action.
      ii. Situations that require the user to make a decision about what actions to take next. This is especially likely if scrolling is required to take the action.
   b. For goals that involve many steps, break the end goal into subgoals. This action has a secondary benefit: when other tasks are to be evaluated in the future, the subgoals may be components of these tasks.
3. After identifying the operations that are required, determine which of the time and motion behaviors just described are necessary for each of the operations.
4. Add the times together to determine the predicted total time that an average expert user would take to reach the goal state.

Variations:

- CogTools (http://cogtool.hcii.cs.cmu.edu/) was created as an electronic alternative to GOMS. It can be used to evaluate the user interface and will provide time estimates. It is highly regarded but will likely appeal to more technically inclined usability specialists.

Example. Figure 5-17 shows how GOMS can be used to predict the time it would take an experienced user to enter the blood pressure for the current patient. As a reminder, the time values come from the list previously presented.

Summary. GOMS provides valuable feedback on the estimated time it takes users to perform specific functions. This can be invaluable for measuring the benefit to users of different methods for interacting with the system, as well as for comparing the appli-

Seq #	Goal	Operation	Code	Category	Time (ms)
	Main Goal: Enter blood pressure (BP) of 160/120 for current patient.				
1	Subgoal: Go to Vital Signs data entry screen.	Recall location of blood pressure data entry.	CP	Cognitive processing	70
2		Locate the Vital Signs tab.	EF	Eye fixation	203
3		Move the mouse pointer to the Vital Signs tab.	MP	Motor processing	70
4		Click on the tab.	MP	Motor processing	70
5	Subgoal: Enter the BP values.	Recognize the new screen.	PP	Perceptual processing	100
6		Recall that "New Vitals" button takes you to pop-up for entering BP.	CP	Cognitive processing	70
7		Locate the "New Vitals" button.	EF	Eye fixation	203
8		Move the mouse pointer to the "New Vitals" button.	MP	Motor processing	70
9		Click on the button.	MP	Motor processing	70
10		Recognize the "Select Encounter" pop-up.	PP	Perceptual processing	100
11		Remember to click on the "New Visit" tab.	CP	Cognitive processing	70
12		Move the mouse pointer to the "New Visit" tab.	MP	Motor processing	70
13		Click on the "New Visit" tab.	MP	Motor processing	70
14		Remember to click on the correct location.	CP	Cognitive processing	70
15		Move the mouse pointer to the correct location name.	MP	Motor processing	70
16		Click on the location.	MP	Motor processing	70
17		Verify that location is correct.	CP	Cognitive processing	70
18		Scan the screen for completeness.	PP	Perceptual processing	100
19		Locate the "Select" button.	EF	Eye fixation	203
20		Move the mouse pointer to the "Select" button.	MP	Motor processing	70
21		Click on the button.	MP	Motor processing	70
22		Locate the "B/P" text entry field.	EF	Eye fixation	203
23		Move the mouse pointer to the text entry field.	MP	Motor processing	70
24		Click in the text field.	MP	Motor processing	70
25		Move hand from mouse to keyboard.	MP	Motor processing	70
26		Type the string "160/120."	MP	Motor processing	490
27		Verify string is correct.	CP	Cognitive processing	70
28		Remember that other fields are optional.	CP	Cognitive processing	70
29		Decide that text entry is complete.	CP	Cognitive processing	70
30		Move hand from keyboard to mouse.	MP	Motor processing	70
31		Locate "Save" button.	EF	Eye fixation	203
32		Move mouse pointer to the "Save" button.	MP	Motor processing	70
33		Click on the "Save" button.	MP	Motor processing	70
	Goal reached			TOTAL TIME (ms)	3,485

Figure 5-17: GOMS

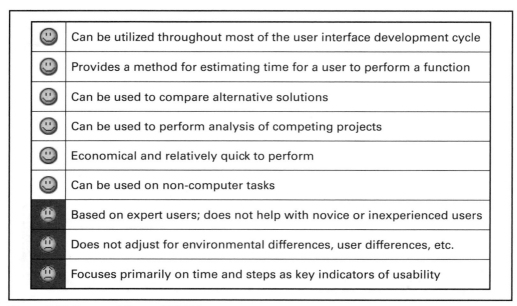

Figure 5-18: Pros and Cons of GOMS

cation with competing products. GOMS is relatively easy to learn, quick to use and requires few resources. Pros and cons for GOMS are outlined in Figure 5-18.

For technical users, CogTools (http://cogtool.hcii.cs.cmu.edu/) is a free tool that provides the same type of information that one gets from manually performing a GOMS assessment. Once it is learned, it allows for users to quantify differences in changes to the user interface. However, the biggest advantage is that it takes much of the human variability out of the process.

Heuristic Evaluation
Description. Touted as "one of the main discount usability engineering methods"[32, p 25] in Nielsen's landmark tome, *Usability Inspection Methods,* heuristic evaluation remains a very popular method for evaluating usability. As the name implies, the process is based on heuristics or "rules of thumb." The process is easy to learn, easy to use, inexpensive and provides quick feedback.

The general idea is that expert evaluators are to independently evaluate the target application against the heuristic principles. Violations of the heuristic principles are identified and classified according to severity, typically on a scale ranging from 1 (cosmetic) to 4 (catastrophic). The violations are compiled into a single document that has the number of evaluators that agreed on each violation, as well as their severity rating. The resulting document can be used by potential users to evaluate an application under consideration or by software development groups to identify and prioritize defects in their application.

There are several examples of usability heuristics: Nielsen's 10 Usability Heuristics,[33] Shneiderman's Eight Golden Rules,[29,34] Connell's[30] Full Principles Set,[35] Gerhardt-Powals[10] Cognitive Engineering Principles,[36,37] and Tognazzini's[17] First Principles of Interaction Design.[38] We are biased in favor of Zhang's 14 Usability Heuristics,[39] in large part because of the work that Dr. Zhang has done in the EHR domain.

Conducting a Heuristic Evaluation

Participants: The number of evaluators varies, depending on their experience performing heuristic evaluations, but five people is considered a reasonable number.[40]

Materials:
- A paper or electronic form to make notes of heuristic violations
- A copy of the heuristic guidelines for reference for each evaluator. A copy of Zhang's 14 Heuristics that includes short word tags in brackets and cues or hints for the main heuristics are included in Figure 5-19.[39]

A sample form using a simple Excel spreadsheet, which can be used to record the heuristic violations, can be found in Figure 5-20. Using Excel is convenient because it simplifies the task of combining separate worksheets, as well as counting and calculating average severity.

Process:

With your form for tracking actions ready for use, we will return to the heuristic evaluation process…

1. Have the evaluators work independently. Discourage sharing information until the evaluations have been completed.
2. Evaluators should go through the scenario twice: the first time to familiarize themselves with the application and the second time to focus more closely on the specific elements of the user interface.
3. If the application relies on domain-specific knowledge and the evaluators do not have domain knowledge, a domain expert can provide support to the evaluators. The domain experts should limit their interactions to domain-specific issues.
4. Evaluators should not be given assistance during the evaluation unless they are unable to proceed. They should ensure that any usability problems are documented before help is provided.
5. The evaluators should go through the scenario, inspecting the user interface and referring to the heuristic principles. Whenever a concern is identified, it should be documented to include identifying the screen where the problem is found, a description of the issue (and why it is an issue) and the severity of the issue. When the evaluator has a recommendation as to how an identified issue can be ameliorated, this should also be documented.
6. After all evaluations have been completed, the forms should be compiled into a single list. Each item should include a count showing how many evaluators identified the issue. For these cases, the average severity should be calculated.

Variations:
- Have the evaluators meet together afterward to review and discuss the items that have been identified.
- Utilize and annotate screen captures or recordings during the evaluation. These allow the development team to more easily discern where the problems occur and identify the elements on the screen that are viewed as heuristic violations.

1. **[Consistency] Consistency and standards.** Users should not have to wonder whether different words, situations or actions mean the same thing. Standards and conventions in product design should be followed.
   a. Sequences of actions (skill acquisition)
   b. Color (categorization)
   c. Layout and position (spatial consistency)
   d. Font, capitalization (levels of organization)
   e. Terminology (delete, del; remove, rm) and language (words, phrases)
   f. Standards (e.g., blue underlined text for unvisited hyperlinks)
2. **[Visibility] Visibility of system state.** Users should be informed about what is going on with the system through appropriate feedback and display of information.
   a. What is the current state of the system?
   b. What can be done at current state?
   c. Where can users go?
   d. What change is made after an action?
3. **[Match] Match between system and world.** The image of the system perceived by users should match the model the users have about the system.
   a. User model matches system image.
   b. Actions provided by the system should match actions performed by users.
   c. Objects on the system should match objects of the task.
4. **[Minimalist] Minimalist.** Any extraneous information is a distraction and a slow-down.
   a. Less is more.
   b. Simple is not equivalent to abstract and general.
   c. Simple is efficient.
   d. Progressive levels of detail
5. **[Memory] Minimize memory load.** Users should not be required to memorize a lot of information to carry out tasks. Memory load reduces users' capacity to carry out the main tasks.
   a. Recognition vs. recall (e.g., menu vs. commands)
   b. Externalize information through visualization
   c. Perceptual procedures
   d. Hierarchical structure
   e. Default values
   f. Concrete examples (DD/MM/YYYY, e.g., 10/20/2013)
   g. Generic rules and actions (e.g., drag objects)
6. **[Feedback] Informative feedback.** Users should be given prompt and informative feedback about their actions.
   a. Information that can be directly perceived, interpreted and evaluated
   b. Levels of feedback (novice and expert)
   c. Concrete and specific, not abstract and general
   d. Response time
      i.   0.1 s for instantaneously reacting
      ii. 1.0 s for uninterrupted flow of thought
      iii. 10 s for the limit of attention
7. **[Flexibility] Flexibility and efficiency.** Users always learn and users are always different. Give users the flexibility of creating customization and shortcuts to accelerate their performance.
   a. Shortcuts for experienced users
   b. Shortcuts or macros for frequently used operations

Figure 5-19: Zhang's 14 Heuristics *(Reprinted from Journal of Biomedical Informatics, 36/1, Zhang J, Johnson TR, Patel VL, Paige DL, Kubose T. Using usability heuristics to evaluate safety of medical devices, 23-30, 2003, with permission from Elsevier.)*

c. Skill acquisition through chunking

d. Examples:

    i. Abbreviations, function keys, hot keys, command keys, macros, aliases, templates, type-ahead, bookmarks, hot links, history, default values, etc.

8. **[Message] Good error messages.** Messages should be informative enough such that users can understand the nature of errors, learn from errors, and recover from errors.

    a. Phrased in clear language, avoid obscure codes. Example of obscure code: "system crashed, error code 147."

    b. Precise, not vague or general. Example of general comment: "Cannot open document."

    c. Constructive

    d. Polite. Examples of impolite message: "illegal user action," "job aborted," "system was crashed," "fatal error," etc.

9. **[Error] Prevent errors.** It is always better to design interfaces that prevent errors from happening in the first place.

    a. Interfaces that make errors impossible

    b. Avoid modes (e.g., vi, text wrap). Or use informative feedback (e.g., different sounds)

    c. Execution error vs. evaluation error

    d. Various types of slips and mistakes

10. **[Closure] Clear closure.** Every task has a beginning and an end. Users should be clearly notified about the completion of a task.

    a. Clear beginning, middle and end

    b. Complete seven stages of actions

    c. Clear feedback to indicate goals are achieved and current stacks of goals can be released. Examples of good closures include many dialogues.

11. **[Undo] Reversible actions.** Users should be allowed to recover from errors. Reversible actions also encourage exploratory learning.

    a. At different levels: a single action, a subtask or a complete task

    b. Multiple steps

    c. Encourage exploratory learning.

    d. Prevent serious errors.

12. **[Language] Use users' language.** The language should be always presented in a form understandable by the intended users.

    a. Use standard meanings of words.

    b. Specialized language for specialized group

    c. User-defined aliases

    d. Users perspective. Example: "We have bought four tickets for you" (bad) vs. "You bought four tickets" (good).

13. **[Control] Users in control.** Do not give users the impression that they are controlled by the systems.

    a. Users are initiators of actors, not responders to actions.

    b. Avoid surprising actions, unexpected outcomes, tedious sequences of actions, etc.

14. **[Document] Help and documentation.** Always provide help when needed.

    a. Context-sensitive help

    b. Four types of help

        i. Task-oriented

        ii. Alphabetically ordered

        iii. Semantically organized

        iv. Search

    c. Help embedded in contents

Figure 5-19 *(Continued)*

Evaluator:

Scenario:

Item #	Location	Description	Heuristic Principle	Average Severity
1				
2				
3				
4				
5				
6				
7				
8				
9				
10				
11				
12				
13				
14				
15				
16				
17				
18				
19				
20				

Figure 5-20: Form for Recording Heuristic Evaluations

Example. Figure 5-21 provides an example from Zhang et al's article, which describes the results of a heuristic evaluation done on an infusion pump.[39]

Summary. Investing in heuristic evaluation as a tool will provide a worthwhile payback. Figure 5-22 details the pros and cons of heuristic evaluations. The method is distinguished for being low cost, quick to implement and providing valuable feedback on the user interface. Using expert evaluators increases the likelihood of finding the most usability issues with the interface.

Because heuristic evaluations do not require using the application, they can be done during the design stage of the user interface. An equally valuable use of heuristic evaluations is to identify user interface concerns when evaluating potential products for purchase; heuristic evaluations can help identify user interfaces that may prove frustrating to users and impede product acceptance.

Evaluator:

Scenario:

Item #	Location	Description	Heuristic Principle	Average Severity
1	Physical design	Tubing is difficult to install. Specifically, the clamp mechanism does not indicate which end goes into pump.	Error, Flexibility	3.25
2	Physical design	The start button may be confused with the ON button; and the stop button may be confused with the OFF button. The meaning of "open" is not obvious.	Error	3
3	Physical design	Start button too close to power button.	Error	3.25
4	Physical design	Contrast adjustment is hidden on the rear of pump handle. It may be inadvertently adjusted when handling pump, and it is hard to find it to adjust it back to normal.	Memory, Visibility	3.75
5	Opening screen	Displayed for only 15 s. During the first few seconds, no actions are available. After self-test, actions become available; user may not notice this change.	Visibility, Error, Consistency	2.5
6	Opening screen	Once the next screen is selected (or appears), users cannot return to internal check/opening screen. To go back, the pump must be turned off.	Undo	3.25
7	Select a Pump Personality	If a personality is highlighted and the select hotkey is pressed, the system immediately enters the Main Display. There is no way to undo selection without turning pump off.	Consistency, Feedback	2.75
8	Infusion Modes and Features	Erratic use of bolding. Some items in bold can be scrolled to and selected, others indicate states and cannot be selected.	Consistency, Minimalist	1.75
9	Main Display	When "Downstream Occlusion" Alarm sounds, if the occlusion is cleared, the infusion begins automatically. If any button is pressed, including Silence Alarm, user must reenter programming screen (by either pressing primary hotkey or Rate or Vol buttons) and press start.	Error, Closure, Consistency, Visibility, Match	3
10	Main Display	Black bar near the bottom of the screen with the message to "press primary or piggyback" in small font. Visibility may be a problem.	Consistency, Visibility, Feedback	2

Figure 5-21: Completed Form Recording Heuristic Violations *(Reprinted from Journal of Biomedical Informatics, 36/1, Zhang J, Johnson TR, Patel VL, Paige DL, Kubose T. Using usability heuristics to evaluate safety of medical devices, 23-30, 2003, with permission from Elsevier.)*

☺	Easy to learn, easy to use
☺	No expensive equipment
☺	Relatively quick to conduct a heuristic evaluation
☺	Provides prompt feedback
☺	Typically identifies cosmetic to serious issues with the user interface
☹	Results are better with expert evaluators
☹	Does not identify what is good about the user interface
☹	Results are not repeatable; there is variance among the findings of the evaluators
☹	Does not address whether the application provides the desired functionality
☹	Expert evaluators may not be readily or cheaply available

Figure 5-22: Pros and Cons of Heuristic Evaluation

Healthcare Failure Mode Effect Analysis (HFMEA)

Designed by the Department of Veterans Affairs' National Center for Public Safety (NCPS), Healthcare Failure Mode Effect Analysis is a five-step process used by healthcare teams to evaluate healthcare processes. HFMEA evolved from engineering's Failure Mode and Effects Analysis, a process intended to pre-emptively identify potential failures in systems and allow for corrective actions. For organizations looking for a tool to use in conducting proactive risk assessments to satisfy the Joint Commission requirement, the HFMEA is an ideal tool.[41]

The Five-Step Process[41]:

1. Define the HFMEA topic—The topic should be tightly focused to enable a thorough examination of the collateral and subordinate components of the topic.
2. Assemble a multidisciplinary team—The team should include domain experts, as well as individuals who are new to the process being examined.
3. Graphically describe the process—Flow diagrams are the recommended method for diagramming. The diagrams should show labels for all steps for easy reference, and complex processes may be broken into subprocesses to manage complexity.
4. Conduct a hazard analysis—Identify failure mode causes, estimate probability and severity for each potential failure mode, and determine if corrective actions should be taken. Tools are available from NCPS to support these activities.
5. Actions and outcome measures—After deciding on an action plan, identify measures to evaluate the new processes.

Conducting an HFMEA

Participants: The team composition is tied to the complexity of the issue being addressed. As noted earlier, subject matter experts as well as people who are not experienced in the domain should be included.

Materials:
- Worksheets are available from the NCPS to facilitate conducting HFMEA evaluations.
  - Microsoft Word version: http://www.patientsafety.va.gov/SafetyTopics/HFMEA/Worksheets.doc
  - Microsoft Excel version for Steps 4 and 5: http://www.patientsafety.va.gov/SafetyTopics/HFMEA/FMEAblkwsheet.xls

Process:
1. Define the topic that will be examined. Examples in healthcare include[42]:
   a. Potential vulnerabilities with existing blood glucose monitoring procedures.
   b. Patient flow through the Emergency Department to reduce overcrowding.
   c. Magnetic resonance imaging (MRI) safety to reduce the threats to equipment, staff and patients.
   d. Evacuation of patients from a VA medical facility in the event of a complete power outage.
2. Identify the personnel who will participate in the HFMEA.
3. Diagram the process. To expedite this process, it is recommended that a draft be completed before the team meeting. The diagram can be polished during the team meeting.
   a. Ensure that the diagrams reflect the actual work processes, not idealized processes.
4. Using the worksheets, analyze the hazards. Provided next are some suggestions that might improve this process[43, p. 584]:
   a. Failure modes are best thought of as anything that can go wrong.
   b. The "what" is less important than the "why" when something goes wrong because this question leads participants to think about prevention and correction.
   c. Descriptions of the problem should suggest how the problem can be mitigated, such as "Because the generator was not actually used during trial runs, there was no way to identify the bad transfer switch until the hospital tried to run off the generator."
   d. Once the team has diagrammed a process, post the flow charts in the work area. Staff on other shifts who do not serve on the team may have ideas for additional steps that have been forgotten or failure modes that no one has suggested.
5. Continuing to use the worksheets as tools, develop corrective actions and an action plan for how to implement the corrective actions. The action plan should be sufficiently detailed to enable ownership of each step to be known and progress to be tracked.

Variations:

- Post diagrams where there is widespread access to them by other staff, along with information about how that staff can contribute ideas that might have been overlooked.
- After the team develops the process diagram, have team members visit the work area to observe staff performing the process and verify that their assumptions are correct.[43, p. 584]

Example. Figure 5-23 is an example illustrating Steps 3 and 4 in an HFMEA evaluation of bar code medication administration (BCMA).[44]

1. Describe the process graphically.

Summary. Its evolution from accepted engineering roots lends HFMEA a level of credibility in problem solving usability issues that is outside the scope of other methods addressed in this section of the book. HFMEA has been part of the medical community's tool set for many years to address threats to patient safety. Often these threats to patient safety come in the form of poor usability.

The role of HFMEA in usability comes from its ability to uncover ways in which user interfaces to EHRs and medical devices can contribute to unwanted outcomes. Examples include identifying option lists in drop-down boxes that are so lengthy users will be less discriminating in the choices they make or, similarly, perform medication calculations incorrectly. Figure 5-24 outlines the pros and cons of HFMEA.

Keystroke-Level Model

Description. Keystroke-Level Model was developed by Card, Moran and Newell in the late 1970s as a method of quantifying performance without requiring complicated or extensive experiments and hand timings.[45] While their technique was developed during the heyday of character-based interfaces, the method has held up as a way to determine performance metrics with today's graphical interfaces.

As originally proposed by Card, Moran and Newell, the technique uses six codes with corresponding timings to represent interface activities (Figure 5-25).

Additionally, Card, Moran and Newell also incorporated the following set of rules for the application of the Mental (M) operator.[45, p. 400]

Begin with a method of encoding that includes all physical operations and response operations. Use Rule 0 to place candidate **M**s, and then cycle through Rules 1 to 4 for each M to see whether it should be deleted.

- **Rule 0**—Insert **M**s in front of all **K**s that are not part of argument strings proper (e.g., text strings or numbers). Place **M**s in front of all **P**s that select commands (not arguments).
- **Rule 1**—If an operator following an **M** is fully anticipated in the operator just previous to **M**, then delete the **M** (e.g., **PMK ~ PK**).
- **Rule 2**—If a string of **MK**s belongs to a cognitive unit (e.g., the name of a command), then delete all **M**s but the first.
- **Rule 3**—If a **K** is a redundant terminator (e.g., the terminator of a command immediately following the terminator of its argument), then delete the **M** in front of the **K**.

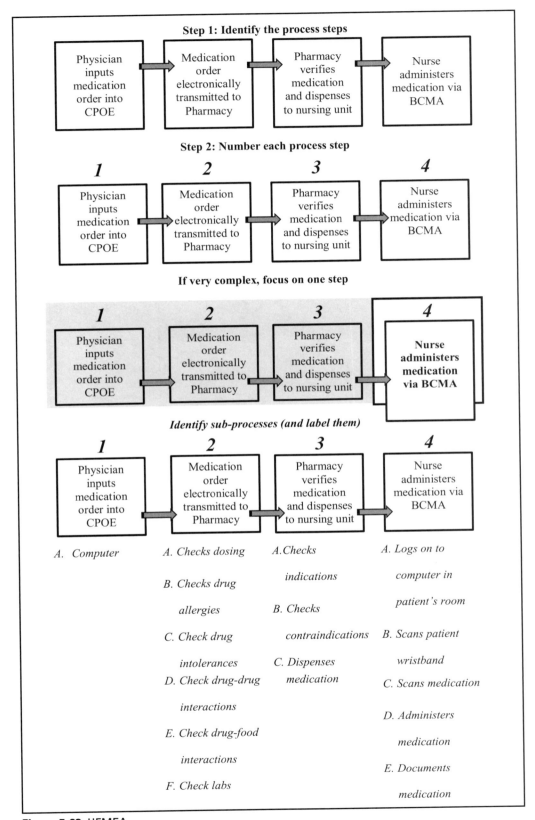

Figure 5-23: HFMEA

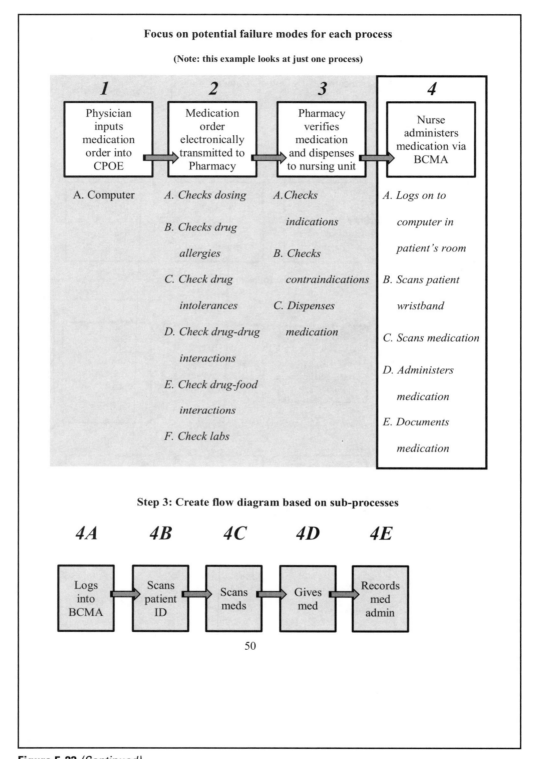

Figure 5-23 *(Continued)*

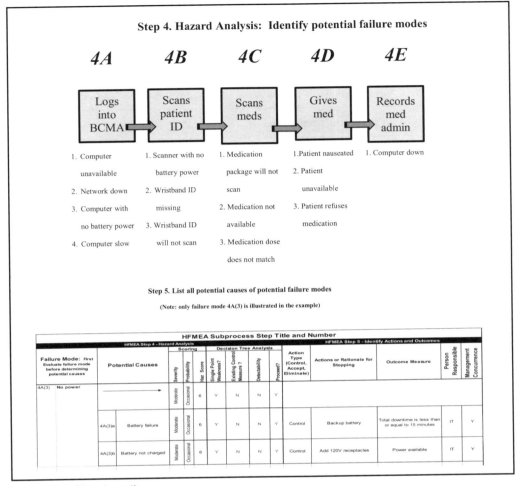

Figure 5-23 *(Continued)*

- **Rule 4**—If a **K** terminates a constant string (e.g., a command name), then delete the **M** in front of the **K**; but if the **K** terminates a variable string (e.g., an argument string), then keep the **M**.

Kieras has proposed the following set of enhanced codes[46] derived from Card, Moran and Newell's work that have been well accepted and which users should find more suitable for modern user interfaces.

Conducting a KLM

Participants: KLM can be performed by a single participant.

Materials:

- Pencil and paper to record the actions to be performed

Process:

The following process can be used with either set of codes presented in Figure 5-25 or Figure 5-26.

1. Choose a representative scenario.
2. Identify how you expect users will perform the scenario.

☺	Effective at identifying root causes and corrective actions of potential and actual problems
☺	Does not require special or expensive equipment
☺	Develops analytical skills in participants; participants get better over time
☺	Capable of engaging all levels of staff
☺	Recognized by users as effective process
☹	Requires moderate level of discipline to be successful
☹	Team activities typically require skilled moderator to avoid inefficient digressions
☹	Should have management support before engaging staff to ensure results will be employed

Figure 5-24: Pros and Cons of HFMEA

Code	Represents	Average Time (secs)*
K	(K)eystroke or mouse press	0.28
P	(P)ointing to a target with a mouse or similar pointing device	1.10
H	(H)oming the hands to the keyboard or to the mouse	0.40
M	(M)entally preparing for executing physical actions	1.35
R	(R)esponse by the system	The time is a function of the system, but is typically not recorded if less than "M" (1.35 sec)
D	(D)rawing straight line segments	*(This activity is not a key concept for EHRs.)*

* Note: The listed timing values represent the times of an average user. The value can fluctuate, depending on many factors, but these values are viable for most scenarios.

Figure 5-25: Interface Activities: KLM Codes and Timing

3. List each action at the keystroke level that is necessary for a user to perform the scenario.
4. For each action in the list:
   a. Identify the corresponding physical operators.
   b. If the user must wait for the system, add operators for these steps.
   c. Insert mental operators (**M**) for actions that require the user to consider his or her just-completed action, to think about what to do next or to make a decision.
5. Add the execution times for each operator.

Code	Represents	Average Time (secs)*
K	(K)eystroke or mouse press. Each character in a string of letters is assigned the same value.	0.28
P	(P)ointing to a target with a mouse or similar pointing device	1.10
B	Press or release the mouse (b)utton	0.10
BB	Click the mouse button (i.e., press and release)	0.20
H	(H)oming the hands to the keyboard or to the mouse	0.40
M	(M)entally preparing for executing physical actions	1.20
W(*t*)	Waiting for the system	The time (*t*) must be determined for each system and activity.

* Note: As noted previously, the listed timing values represent the times of an average user. The value can fluctuate depending on many factors, but these values are viable for most scenarios.

Figure 5-26: KLM Codes[46]

6. Total the execution times. This yields the estimated time it will take an expert user to complete the scenario.

Variations:

- Use a spreadsheet or similar electronic tool to record actions and sum the numbers.
- Measure only keystrokes. This simplification is noticeably less accurate when the task is not tilted substantially in favor of keystroke actions.[45]
- Use a constant for the **M** operator and then prorate this value against all physical operators. Again, this is also less accurate as Card's rules lead to improved accuracy.
- Measure the times for representative users and use these newly defined values for timing. This could be useful if, for example, the typical users are highly skilled typists.

Example. The following example (Figure 5-27) was developed by Saitwal, Feng, Walji, Patel and Zhang for their evaluation of an EHR. This subset is from their scenario of reviewing the coding of a medical encounter.[47, p. 503] It has been slightly modified to include the operator name in the description and to reflect Kieras codes and timings, most notably on Action 8.

Summary. Figure 5-28 outlines the pros and cons to KLM. The model for measuring performance allows users to evaluate performance of applications in a standardized way. It does not predict how common users will perform, but the results allow for uniform timing measurements of user scenarios. KLM can be used during early development of the user interface as soon as it is possible to determine how actions would be performed. By measuring as-is timings against to-be timings, KLM also can be used to

Action #	Description	Operators	Time(s)
1	Mental—think of location in main menu	M	1.2
2	Home—move the hand to the mouse	H	0.4
3	Point—move the mouse pointer to the Go option in the main menu	P	1.1
4	Point—move the mouse to patient	P	1.1
5	Mental—recall the name of the patient	M	1.2
6	Mental—locate the desired patient name in the list	M	1.2
7	Point—move the mouse pointer to the desired patient name	P	1.1
8	Click—click on the desired patient name	BB	0.2
	TOTAL		**7.5**

Figure 5-27: KLM

🙂	Enables consistent easily understood performance measures
🙂	Can be used to evaluate performance of contending methods to perform a task
🙂	Can also be used to compare performance against competing products
🙂	Is simple to plan and perform
🙁	Only performance is measured
🙁	Does not predict how users will actually perform a task
🙁	Is an estimate based on expert users; results cannot be used to predict performance of common users
🙁	Accurately incorporating mental operators is more complicated

Figure 5-28: Pros and Cons of KLM

measure whether changes to an application will result in improved performance. It is important to realize that KLM is based on how an expert user would perform the identified sequence of actions; it does not take into account typing mistakes, user skill levels, familiarity with the application or other factors that influence actual user performance.

Prototyping

Description. It is hard to overstate the value of prototyping to the usability enthusiast. Although prototyping is not a usability methodology *per se* for professional development shops, prototyping is the foundation for creating usable systems. Prototyping refers to the process of creating a mockup of the user interface that enables viewers or designers to envision how people will interact with the system. Mockups can range from simple sketches to realistic models of the user interface that allow for user interactions.

In addition to being able to perform usability evaluations with prototypes, they serve as valuable visual models that enable purposeful communications among designers, developers and customers or end users. All too often, requirements are developed based on input from customers or end users. However, it is not at all uncommon to show end users the user interface design only to learn that they had a different picture in their mind from the same requirements. Prototypes help alleviate this by allowing the user interface designer to quickly create screens that can be previewed with the end user. If the designs are off-the-mark, changes can be made much more easily to the prototype than to screens that have been developed by programming.

As mentioned previously, prototypes can range from sketches to realistic, interactive models. Experienced user interface developers will frequently advise that initial prototypes be created in low fidelity (which is the "sketchy" look), rather than looking too realistic, as the realism can distract viewers from the screen flows and overall presentation by having them focus on colors and button styles and fonts and such.

Prototyping software is available from a variety of vendors and in a range of prices. Because this is a competitive product field, readers are encouraged to read online reviews to see which products are garnering the most positive reviews. Personal experiences with Balsamiq (http://www.balsamiq.com), GUI Design Studio (http://www.carettasoftware.com) and Axure (http://www.axure.com) have been positive, but there are other products with ardent supporters. At the time of this writing, http://c2.com/cgi/wiki?GuiPrototypingTools maintains an informal list of products and some brief bullet points for each for those who want to survey the different offerings.

Conducting a Prototype

Participants: One

Materials:
- Requirements that describe the desired functionality and an understanding of the target user characteristics are important in creating a prototype.

Process:
The process of designing a prototype is beyond the scope of this book. Readers are referred to any of the numerous books or websites on user interface design for guidance. Because of the importance of prototypes, we want to show some different mockups of the OpenVista community version home screen to illustrate how well prototypes can mimic real programs.

Examples. In this section, you will first be presented with a reference screen shot from the Patient Summary screen of the OpenVista© application (Figure 5-29), an open-source EHR available from Medsphere (http://www.medsphere.org), followed by two screens that have been created with software prototyping tools.

The next screen shot (Figure 5-30) was created using Balsamiq (http://www.balsamiq.com), a well-known low-fidelity, low-cost tool that has a popular following. You will notice that the lines look more hand drawn and the fonts have a more casual appearance. Consequently, this screen does not look like a screen found in commercial applications. However, as a low-fidelity image, it can be created easily and it effectively

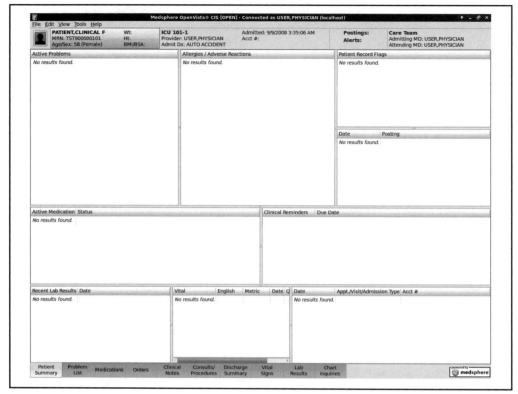

Figure 5-29: OpenVista© Patient Summary Screen

conveys the look of the application so designers can get feedback from users or can use the mockup to conduct evaluations of the interface.

Figure 5-31 was created using Prototyper Pro by JustInMind (http://www. justinmind.com). Higher-end software tools like Prototyper Pro enable designers to create mockups that behave much like a true program. Designers can connect them to data so the contents of onscreen tables can be selectively updated, forms can accept and validate input, screens can dynamically update and users can save creations to be reused in subsequent screens or even other projects. And in what seems a bit like an ironic twist, the designers can tell the application to draw screens to look like they are hand drawn. These are versatile and powerful tools for constructing prototypes.

Summary. Prototypes are the power tools of usability evaluations. They enable users and stakeholders to see the vision of the user interface and to describe what they like and dislike. Prototypes also allow designers to validate their designs against end-user requirements and to tweak the design where discrepancies are identified. And because the user interface can be modeled with prototypes, it is possible to conduct many types of usability evaluations without utilizing programmers to create working code. Additionally, the programmers benefit because instead of having to design a user interface that may or may not be what is expected, they get to implement a design that has the "stamp of approval" from the users and stakeholders. Figure 5-32 outlines the pros and cons of using prototypes.

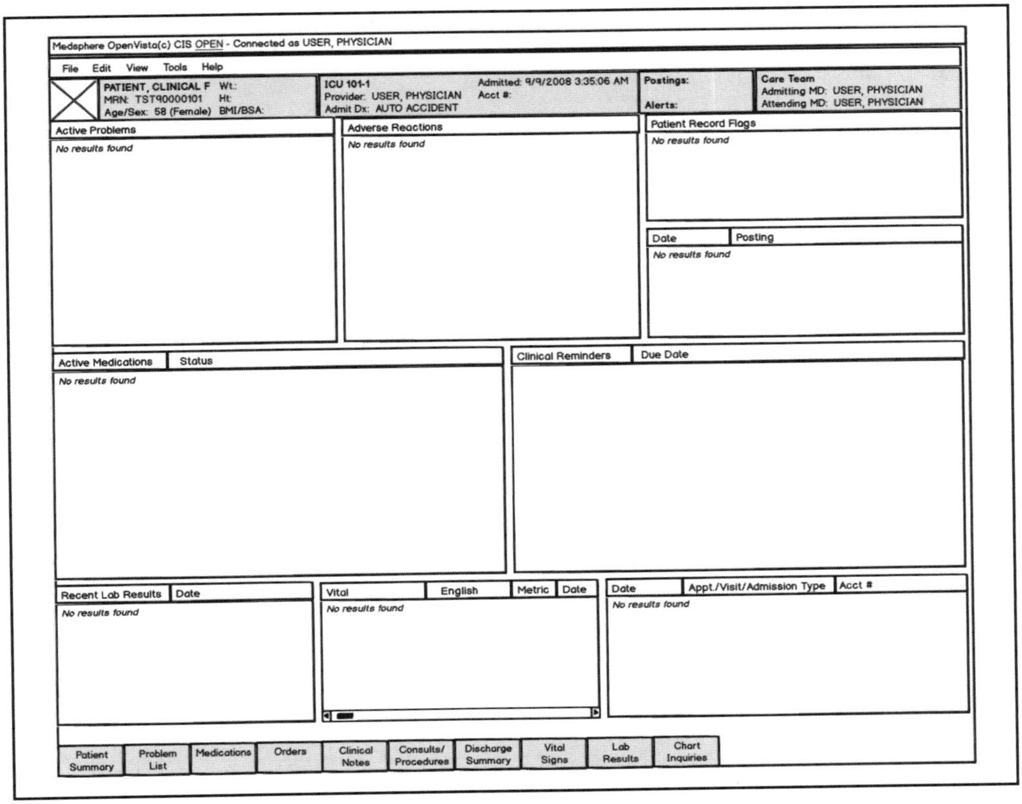

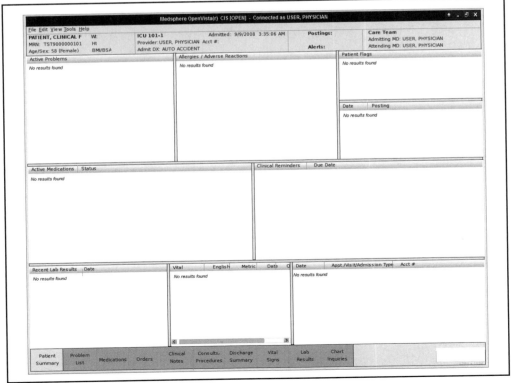

Figure 5-30: Low-Resolution Mockup Created with Balsamiq

Figure 5-31: High-Fidelity Mockup Created with Prototyper Pro

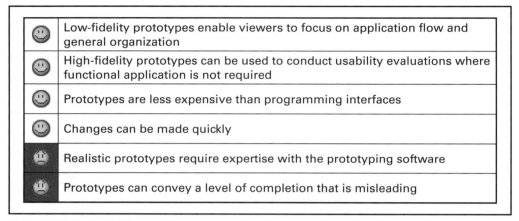

Figure 5-32: Pros and Cons of Prototypes

Satisfaction Surveys

Description. Satisfaction surveys provide usability evaluations with an efficient way to gather self-reported data from users about their experience with the application. Surveys can help the usability expert identify areas that are pleasing to users, as well as those that draw their ire. Compelling information can be reliably developed from a well-designed survey.

Users can be surveyed in a variety of ways, including open-ended interviews and short-answer questions. However, Likert surveys, which are based on, for example, a five-point or seven-point set of responses, are commonly used because they are convenient to conduct, data can be readily collected and processed electronically, and there are a number of these types of surveys that have been statistically validated. Contributing to the attractiveness of Likert surveys is the ability to offer them using online services, like SurveyMonkey.com, QuestionPro.com, and Zoomerang.com, which provide full-service capabilities from hosting the survey, to compiling the data, to providing analytics based on the data.[48]

Conducting a Satisfaction Survey

Participants: One person can manage a survey program

Materials:

- Choose the survey that fits with the goals of your project. While experienced usability experts may choose to create their own surveys, using an existing survey offers the assurance that it meets the statistical requirements of being reliable and valid. These are important if the results are to be shared with others or there is a wish to draw conclusions about the members of the population who are not participating in the survey.

Process:

1. The first step is to identify the goals of the survey. What attributes of the user experience is the survey expected to measure?
2. Choose who the information will be coming from; who is part of the sample? There are three common sampling approaches[48]:

    a. Census sampling is when everyone in the target group is surveyed. For example, all doctors are asked to take a survey on their satisfaction with the EHR.

    b. Judgmental sampling occurs when the participants are selected based on certain criteria, like age or gender, to ensure a desired mix of user attributes or qualities.

    c. Statistical or random sampling is the gold standard, as this allows for conclusions that are drawn from the sample to be generalized to the population from which the sample was drawn. There is a rigor to the process of random sampling that belies the nature of the name "random."

3. Decide how you will be handling people who are chosen to participate but who do not participate for one reason or another. You might be able to have them participate at a later time or you might have to deal with the sample group's makeup being skewed.

4. Determine if the survey will be offered using paper and pencil or electronically. If the survey is being offered electronically, will users be accessing an online form or a form that is local to the computer or mobile device they are using?

5. Depending on the survey method offered, you might need to schedule a room so you can invite participants and reduce the chances that they have competing activities that limit ad hoc participation.

6. After the surveys have been completed, compile the information and analyze it. Depending on your requirements, knowledge and skills, computing basic statistics (mean, median, mode and standard deviation) could prove telling. These are attractive because most people are familiar with them and they can be easily calculated with any spreadsheet software. The demands of some projects will make it necessary to use more advanced statistics. We will not be discussing statistics in this book, as there are numerous resources available online and in recent textbooks.

Variations:

- Surveys may be offered after the completion of each task or after the series of tasks have been completed.
- Consider how user training affects survey responses by choosing samples from members of the population who have been trained and members of the population who have not been trained.
- Other EHR attributes that could be of interest are visual appeal, impact on efficiency, usefulness, ease of navigation and responsiveness.[49]
- Engage nontechnical stakeholders to ensure diverse ideas.

Example: Following are examples of surveys that are generally available. For the usability evaluator with access to computers, Gary Perlman has created a website (http://oldwww.acm.org/perlman/question.html) that enables these questionnaires and others to be offered via the Internet; the results can be emailed back to the usability evaluators. Be aware that there are some technical skills required to get the most use of the web-based questionnaires on the Perlman webpage.

    The *System Usability Scale* (SUS) was developed over 25 years ago, and it continues to be widely used. The survey is scored by assigning a value of 0 to 4 for each item. For items 1, 3, 5, 7 and 9, the value corresponds to their response minus 1, so a "Strongly

Disagree," which is a "1," is scored as 1-1=0. Similarly, "Strongly Agree" or "5" is scored as 5-1=4. Because of a different wording, items 2, 4, 6, 8 and 10 are scored by subtracting their value from 5. So for question 2, "Strongly Agree" or "5" is scored as 5-5=0.[49]

		Strongly disagree				Strongly agree
1.	I think that I would like to use this system frequently.					
		1	2	3	4	5
2.	I found the system unnecessarily complex.					
		1	2	3	4	5
3.	I thought the system was easy to use.					
		1	2	3	4	5
4.	I think I would need the support of a technical person to be able to use this system.					
		1	2	3	4	5
5.	I found the various functions in this system were well integrated.					
		1	2	3	4	5
6.	I thought this system was too inconsistent.					
		1	2	3	4	5
7.	I would imagine that most people would learn to use this system very quickly.					
		1	2	3	4	5
8.	I found the system very cumbersome to use.					
		1	2	3	4	5
9.	I felt very confident using the system.					
		1	2	3	4	5
10.	I needed to learn a lot of things before I could get going with this system.					
		1	2	3	4	5

The Computer System Usability Questionnaire (CSUQ) was developed by IBM in 1993 as part of its effort to develop tools for evaluating system usability. CSUQ has 19 questions, and scoring results in four scores—the total score and three subscale scores. The subscales are: System Usefulness (items 1–8), Information Quality (items 9–15) and Interface Quality (items 16–18). The averages of the total score and the subscores are used for comparisons, where lower scores are better.[50]

1. Overall, I am satisfied with how easy it is to use this system.

STRONGLY AGREE   1   2   3   4   5   6   7   STRONGLY DISAGREE

COMMENTS:

2. It is simple to use this system.

STRONGLY AGREE   1   2   3   4   5   6   7   STRONGLY DISAGREE

COMMENTS:

3. I can effectively complete my work using this system.

STRONGLY AGREE   1   2   3   4   5   6   7   STRONGLY DISAGREE

COMMENTS:

4. I am able to quickly complete my work using this system.

STRONGLY AGREE   1   2   3   4   5   6   7   STRONGLY DISAGREE

COMMENTS:

5. I am able to efficiently complete my work using this system.

STRONGLY AGREE   1   2   3   4   5   6   7   STRONGLY DISAGREE

COMMENTS:

6. I feel comfortable using this system.

STRONGLY AGREE   1   2   3   4   5   6   7   STRONGLY DISAGREE

COMMENTS:

7. It was easy to learn to use this system.

STRONGLY AGREE   1   2   3   4   5   6   7   STRONGLY DISAGREE

COMMENTS:

8. I believe I became productive quickly using this system.

STRONGLY AGREE   1   2   3   4   5   6   7   STRONGLY DISAGREE

COMMENTS:

9.   The system gives error messages that clearly tell me how to fix problems.

STRONGLY   **STRONGLY**
AGREE   1   2   3   4   5   6   7   **DISAGREE**
    COMMENTS:

10. Whenever I make a mistake using the system, I recover easily and quickly.

STRONGLY   **STRONGLY**
AGREE   1   2   3   4   5   6   7   **DISAGREE**
    COMMENTS:

11. The information (such as on-line help, on-screen messages and other documenta-
     tion) provided with this system is clear.

STRONGLY   **STRONGLY**
AGREE   1   2   3   4   5   6   7   **DISAGREE**
    COMMENTS:

12. It is easy to find the information I need.

STRONGLY   **STRONGLY**
AGREE   1   2   3   4   5   6   7   **DISAGREE**
    COMMENTS:

13. The information provided with the system is easy to understand.

STRONGLY   **STRONGLY**
AGREE   1   2   3   4   5   6   7   **DISAGREE**
    COMMENTS:

14. The information is effective in helping me complete my work.

STRONGLY   **STRONGLY**
AGREE   1   2   3   4   5   6   7   **DISAGREE**
    COMMENTS:

15. The organization of information on the system screens is clear.

STRONGLY   **STRONGLY**
AGREE   1   2   3   4   5   6   7   **DISAGREE**
    COMMENTS:

Note: *The interface includes those items that you use to interact with the system. For example, some components of the interface are the keyboard, the mouse, the screens (including their use of graphics and language).*

16. The interface of this system is pleasant.

**STRONGLY
AGREE**   1   2   3   4   5   6   7   **STRONGLY
DISAGREE**

     COMMENTS:

17. I like using the interface of this system.

**STRONGLY
AGREE**   1   2   3   4   5   6   7   **STRONGLY
DISAGREE**

     COMMENTS:

18. This system has all the functions and capabilities I expect it to have.

**STRONGLY
AGREE**   1   2   3   4   5   6   7   **STRONGLY
DISAGREE**

     COMMENTS:

19. Overall, I am satisfied with this system.

**STRONGLY
AGREE**   1   2   3   4   5   6   7   **STRONGLY
DISAGREE**

     COMMENTS:

Summary. Surveys are ideal when looking to gather quantitative usability data. There are existing surveys that have earned the acceptance of the statistical community; they can be offered as pencil and paper or online; they generate data that can be analyzed using readily available software; and when using the proper controls, the results can be generalized to the larger population. If you are looking to identify tan-

🙂	Excellent for developing quantitative research. The data can be analyzed with any respected statistics package, like SPSS or SAS.
🙂	Surveys are available that meet the statistical standards of reliability and validity.
🙂	Surveys can be done easily and quickly. Online surveys further simplify the administration and data compilation.
🙂	If proper sampling techniques are used with a proven survey, the results can be generalized to the bigger population.
🙁	Surveys that do not utilize random sampling techniques cannot be generalized.
🙁	Statistical knowledge is necessary to perform anything other than basic analysis of the results.
🙁	Analysts must be aware if attributes of the population being surveyed change, such as age or technical skills, as these may impact the survey results.
🙁	Developing custom surveys requires expertise to create the survey and to ensure that results are reliable and valid.
🙁	Surveys give a big-picture view of the application's usability; they are not intended to identify individual usability problems.

Figure 5-33: Pros and Cons of Usability Satisfaction Surveys

gible usability issues, consider other methods as surveys tend to assess user attitudes and impressions about qualities of the application. Figure 5-33 on the previous page provides the pros and cons of usability satisfaction surveys.

MORE DIFFICULT USABILITY EVALUATION METHODS

Task Analysis

Description. The goal of task analysis is to identify the behavioral and cognitive steps that users take to complete their work. Furthermore, the task analysis identifies which of the steps are important in completing the work, as opposed to steps that might be called "overhead" because they do not contribute to users getting their work done.[51]

The cognitive aspects of task analysis ask the informaticist to be attentive to how the user formulates mental goal states and the strategies and actions to achieve these goals. Do users rely on internal representations or external representations to guide them through the task? Internal representations are the cognitive signposts that we construct in our minds to remember what to do next; when we memorize a sequence of steps, we have an internal representation of the task. External representations are those things that serve as visual signposts to remind us where to go or what to do. Because they do not tax our memory and in fact ease our mental burden, external representations can make it easier for us to complete our assigned tasks.[52]

It can be helpful to think about task analysis in terms of the initial inputs, the desired output and what happens during the interim steps that changes the input to the desired output or final state. This line of thinking has the benefit of helping the informaticist recognize activities or events that add value by moving the task toward the desired output, as opposed to activities or events that have no discernable impact on advancing toward the desired output or final state of the task.

A top-down approach is often taken in conducting the task analysis; that is, the top-level tasks are identified first. From these top-level tasks, the component subtasks are identified next. This process continues until a base level has been reached. During the task analysis, the informaticist should note the participants, the information or the event that causes the task to start, what information is changed during the task, who makes changes, and what causes the task to transition to another person or state. If the task hierarchy has been created from interviews or by report, then the informaticist is advised to observe the users performing the task to confirm that the documentation of the task reflects what happens.[30,52]

When the task analysis is being conducted on a computer-based application, it can be used to distinguish the best sequence of steps to model the user's work when there are multiple options being considered. In this situation, the steps for each option are detailed, which enables the use of a method like KLM or GOMS to be used to estimate the timing for each option. (Note: These are both described in this section of the book.)

Conducting a Task Analysis

Participants: One informaticist, one or more users who perform the task being analyzed

Materials:

- Pencil and paper, or other method of recording steps

Process:

1. Identify the task to be analyzed.
2. Identify the initial state and the final state or the desired output.
3. Break down the task into subtasks.
   a. Number each step of the subtask in sequence.
   b. For each step of the subtask, collect the following information:
      i. Participants in the subtask
      ii. Required information and resources (and where each originates from)
      iii. Information and resources used, changed or produced by the step
      iv. Is there a measurable item or an event that tells the participants the step has been completed? If not, what tells them that they have completed the step?
   c. If the subtasks are complex, break them into subordinate levels of subtasks until the final level are basic tasks.
4. If the development of the hierarchy of tasks and subtasks was based on reports, observe the tasks to validate the list.
5. Look for steps in the hierarchy of tasks and subtasks that do not make a material contribution to achieving the final state or the desired output. These are candidates for elimination or modification.
6. KLM or GOMS can be used with the results of the task analysis to estimate the times to perform the tasks.

Variations:

- Include details about the cognitive aspects[53]:
  – Internal vs. external representations
  – Other factors that compete for the users' attention or memory
- Identify points in the process at which errors can occur, either due to resource constraints, cognitive issues or environmental factors.
- Create flow diagrams showing the flow of information and resources across participants to complete the work.

Example. Figure 5-34 is an excerpt of the table from Zhang, Patel, Johnson, Chung, and Turley's article on safety and medical devices. They created a table to track the common activities of a task analysis and extended it so they could also track more state

Traditional Task Analysis			Extended Task Analysis				
#	Goal/Method	Operators	Physical State	Current Screen	Internal	External	Error Affordances
1.00	**Prepare Device**						
1.10	Plug in	Insert plug	Plugged in/off/unloaded			See plug	
1.20	Make sure lockout if off	Verify lockout status	Plugged in/off/unloaded		Remember the switch location	Switch on back of device	Possible omission. (intention formation) – not visible
1.30	Turn device on	Press "on/off"	Plugged in/on/unloaded	Self Test – Please Wait		On/off button	
2.00	**Check Mode**						
2.10	If mode acceptable then go to 4.0 If mode is unacceptable go to 5.0	Decide: If mode is acceptable then go to Step 16; if mode is unacceptable then go to Step 13	Plugged in/on/unloaded	'New patient clears stored data'	Remember where and when to look	Presented on display briefly	Can be overlooked; it is only presented for 15 seconds.
…	…	…	…	…	…	…	…

Figure 5-34: The First Steps in Operating an Infusion Pump[53, p.333]

🙂	Identifies functionality necessary to perform the task
🙂	Involves participants in the process
🙂	Provides strong input for requirements development
🙂	Can be used to analyze task options to improve efficiency
🙂	Cognitive extensions contribute to identifying failure possibilities
🙁	Detailing tasks and subtasks can be time consuming
🙁	Not designed to identify user interface deficiencies
🙁	Must be kept current, as tasks are likely to change

Figure 5-35: Pros and Cons of Task Analysis

information and cognitive details. The table has been represented faithfully, except for some wording and minor format changes.[53]

Summary. Task analysis provides insights into the way users work. By examining the work processes, this usability evaluation yields information on the work of each of the participants, as well as the resources required and how the output of the work is produced throughout the task. Understanding the details of the user's work is important when developing initial requirements or when redesigning an application. In addition, when there are two or more possibilities for how a task should be implemented, a task analysis can be used to evaluate the options to determine which model of the task is likely to be the most efficient. Figure 5-35 provides the pros and cons of task analysis.

Think-Aloud Protocol

Description. In trying to understand user behaviors that are different than what was anticipated, software designers, developers and customer support specialists may find themselves asking "What were you thinking?!" The think-aloud protocol, which Nielsen says "may be the single most valuable usability method," is intended to answer this question.[54, p. 195]

The goal of thinking aloud is to provide the usability project members with a qualitative view of the users' experience with the application by having users describe what they are trying to do along with aspects of the user interface that impede or expedite their progress. In the simplest form of think aloud, the usability evaluator asks the user to think aloud while using the application.[54] More complicated implementations incorporate voice and video recording technologies, along with eye-tracking solutions to collect more detailed information about the user behaviors and thought processes.[30]

Conducting a think aloud session can be challenging for the user and usability evaluator. Some users find it difficult to share their thoughts aloud.[55] Others forget to keep talking as they are using the application. Another consideration is that users are more deliberate when engaged in a think aloud session and make more mistakes in using the application than users who are not involved in a think-aloud protocol.[53] To reduce the influence of the usability evaluator on the user, the user must be informed in advance of their responsibility and then the usability evaluator must resist giving advice, encouragement or coaching unless the user is stuck when using the application, or if the user ceases to think aloud, or if the user cannot be heard. In any of these situations, the usability evaluator should strive to keep the dialog with the user to a minimum.[54] The usability evaluator should also ensure that the task being performed matches the user's experience level; avoid asking an experienced user to perform a task better suited for a novice and vice versa.[56,57] It is also useful to explain that understanding how physicians and nurses respond and interact with health IT during the evaluation session will help designers understand how to improve software for their work.[58]

The usability evaluator may be surprised to find that their observations of the users during the think aloud session may not match up with the user's sense of the experience. Segall reported numerous discrepancies, including trouble navigating, difficulty finding information, extensive time to complete tasks, error-prone behaviors and data entry frustrations.[59]

Conducting a Think-Aloud Session

Participants: As a minimum, one user and one usability evaluator. (Usability tests that utilize the think-aloud protocol have shown maximum benefits with five users.[60])

Materials:

- System with the application to be tested and a scenario for the user to perform
- Pencil and paper or suitable electronic devices to record observations
- If the observer is not able to directly view the user, position a mirror so the observer can view the user's facial mannerisms.

Process:

1. Give the user a scenario to perform with the application.
2. Set the user's expectations:
   a. The think-aloud protocol is used to gather information to improve the application; it is NOT a measure of the user's skill or speed.
   b. The user should do the best he or she can to verbalize his or her thoughts.
   c. The usability observer will be there to document the user's thoughts and observe the user's actions.
   d. The usability observer will provide guidance in the event that the user is stuck and unable to proceed. The usability observer is instructed not to give advice, suggestions or criticisms.
3. Observe the user as he goes through the scenario and record what the user is doing with the application and what reactions the user is having. Recording the audio allows the observer to focus on the user's nonverbal behavior. Body language and facial mannerisms can convey information that is lost when the observer is only attending to the user's speech.
   a. Novice or users with no experience in the domain will find it helpful to have a short training session or preview, so they are less likely to get into a situation that reflects more on the user than the application.

Variations:

- Review the session with the user and allow him or her to offer additional comments. This can be especially useful when the session has been recorded and the recording can be played back.
- Have two users work collaboratively on the scenario (referred to as *constructive interaction* by Nielsen). Without some type of recording equipment, the observer can be quickly overwhelmed by the amount of feedback this approach generates; people tend to be more conversational when working together.[54, p. 198]
- Instead of offering minimal guidance, utilize a coach for the user. The user is allowed to ask any questions related to using the system and the coach will address the questions. A benefit of this variation is that it highlights aspects of the interface where the users have more uncertainty or ambiguity.[54, p. 199]
- By coding the notes from the think aloud session using heuristic principles, the findings can be categorized and rated. This can make the results easier to communicate to people who do not have a usability background.

Example. Figure 5-36 highlights some of the comments collected by Li et al. in their study using the think-aloud protocol in a usability evaluation of clinical decision support (CDS).[61, p. 765] The table demonstrates how the think aloud content can be categorized using usability heuristics.

Summary. The think-aloud protocol is an essential tool for usability evaluations. It is a simple, low-tech approach that belies the value it brings. It provides genuine quotable feedback from users about the user interface, which can be exceptionally persuasive. A think aloud session can be conducted without formal testing facilities, and only minimal skills are required of the observer during the session. And by utilizing recording technologies, details that might otherwise be missed can be captured and analyzed. Perhaps the biggest challenge is that some users may need to be excused if they find it intimidating to speak about their thoughts when going through a scenario. Figure 5-37 outlines the pros and cons of think aloud.

MOST DIFFICULT USABILITY EVALUATION METHOD

TURF (Tasks, Users, Representations and Functions)

Description. TURF is a comprehensive framework that targets the analysis, design and evaluation of usability. The framework, originally called "UFuRT," was developed by Jiajie Zhang, PhD, of the School of Biomedical Informatics at the University of Texas Health Science Center in Houston.[62]

As indicated in the topic title, TURF stands for the key concepts which embody the essence of the framework: Tasks, Users, Representations and Functions. It is the combination of these that makes TURF unique and effective. TURF's comprehensive view of usability takes the adherent from understanding the nature of the users to addressing how information can be best presented to the users. We will discuss these in more detail next.

USER. We will start by looking at the user analysis. Users are the foundation for successfully incorporating usability concepts. In the competitive EHR marketplace, a product's survival may depend on having effective, efficient and satisfied users. In the

Code	Definition	Example Coded Statement
USABILITY	Refers to commentary on the perceived effectiveness, efficiency and "ease or lack-of-ease of use" of the iCPR CDS	"It's becoming a lot of clicking and reading and you want to do this thing quickly, especially if you have a lot of patients waiting. . ."
VISIBILITY	Refers to commentary on the extent an image, text or message is noticed or attended to	"I just see that BPA [alert] here. Normally I probably wouldn't see it, since I don't usually look here; but, if it had been more prominent, I might have seen it—if it had popped up."
WORKFLOW	Refers to commentary on the general order and sequence of tasks and activities involved in a patient encounter	"I think it depends on when you start using the tool because if you use it right from the beginning. . .you could get distracted and forget to go through other questions maybe. . .I just think these [order] sets should come when you ask for them, not from the walk-in diagnosis."
CONTENT	Refers to commentary on the content of information provided by the iCPR CDS	"I think the soup issue might be an issue with my patients; we see patients over 50 with hypertension, and we wouldn't really tell them to take chicken soup because it is full of sodium."
UNDERSTAND-ABILITY	Refers to commentary on the extent to which the text within the CDS is comprehendible	"Supportive care is weird [text phrasing] because it is saying pneumonia, and the patient does not have it."
USEFULNESS	Refers to commentary on the extent the tool (and information provided by it) is perceived as helpful during clinical decision making and care delivery. "I don't like this one [order set] as much... I realize this is all about evidence-based medicine... [but] I just think there is more in a clinical picture and this thing is pushing you in a direction without taking into account [the full clinical picture]."	
NAVIGATION	Refers to commentary on the provider's ability to move through the system (i.e., where to go, how to move forward or backward)	"A prompt of some sort would be good. I would need a prompt; I don't know where to go next."

Figure 5-36: Comments Collected from Think Aloud Session *(Reprinted from International Journal of Informatics, 81/11, Li AC, Kannry JL, Kushniruk A, Chrimes D. McGinn TG, Edonyabo D., Mann DM. Integrating usability testing and think-aloud protocol analysis with "near-live" clinical simulations in evaluating clinical decision support, 761-772, 2012, with permission from Elsevier.)*

😊	Low costs, no expensive equipment required
😊	Can be utilized without extensive training
😊	Can be used with all types of interfaces, including devices
😊	Engages users, which results compelling feedback
😟	Is not a good fit with certain users
😟	Not useful for performance evaluations
😟	User behavior is affected by participation
😟	User behavior can be biased by observer interactions

Figure 5-37: Pros and Cons of Think Aloud

realm of EHRs, there are currently more than 3,500 products competing for users.[63] Developing and sustaining a complex product like an EHR is difficult and expensive, so vendors spare no effort trying to attract and retain users. And from the consumer side, the cost of deploying an EHR across a hospital system is staggering, with numerous reports of budgets over $100 million and implementation timelines that span multiple years.[63,64] Because of these high costs, acquiring an EHR system that is poorly received by physicians and other healthcare professionals is guaranteed to bring no less than a hail of nasty comments. All of this points to the importance of understanding the users of the systems.

Within the TURF framework, user attributes are helpful in developing user profiles. Toward this end, the first step is to identify the categories of users. Obviously an EHR will be used by physicians and nurses, but other healthcare professionals and ancillary staff will also be using the EHR. The objective is to identify the relevant attributes of each type of user with the ultimate goal to maximize the benefits to all users.

Gathering information about the following characteristics for each type of user, such as those identified in Figure 5-38, will generate user profiles to guide the designers, developers and evaluators in their decision making.[51]

FUNCTION. Exploring functionality yields a greatly increased awareness of the work domain. With the TURF framework, there are three common ways to look at

User Attributes			
Age-related skills	Gender	Education	Cultural influences
Religious influences	Income	Ethnicity	Language skills
Family influences	Technical skills	Cognitive skills	Physical abilities
Domain knowledge	Time demands		

Figure 5-38: User Attributes

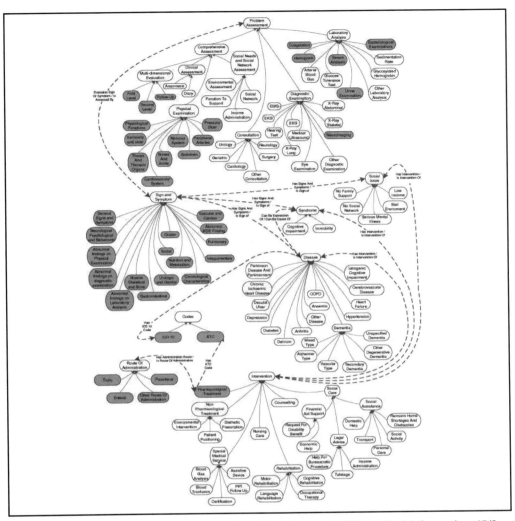

Figure 5-39: Example of an Ontology *(Reprinted from Journal of Biomedical Informatics, 45/3, Riaño D, Real F, López-Vallverdú JA, et al. An ontology-based personalization of health-care knowledge to support clinical decisions for chronically ill patients, 239-246, 2012, with permission from Elsevier.)*

functionality. The first view is to develop a holistic understanding of the work tasks, which results in an ontology. An ontology is an abstract, technology-agnostic way to represent knowledge, items and relationships in a domain. Figure 5-39 is a graphic representation of part of an ontology representing the healthcare concepts associated with the home care of chronically ill patients.[65] While the graphic illustrates the amount of information that a formal ontology contains about a domain, an ontology is equally valuable because it also serves as a reference for information that is not vital to the domain. TURF treats information that is not necessary to the work as *overhead*; items identified as overhead are closely examined to see if they can be eliminated or streamlined. With the ontology created, the usability evaluator has a solid understanding of the entities involved in the work, and their interrelationships and constraints. And this is the basis for identifying nonessential work.

TURF also examines the usefulness of functionality by using three different lenses.[51] The first lens, the DESIGNER model, is the vision of the designer of the system, which is the functionality already built into the system. This view illuminates the entire set of functionality the system provides, which can be a lengthy list for a complex system like an EHR. In the absence of a design or architectural document, creating the list can be done by walking through the application and documenting the operations or functions.

After creating the list of functionality in the system, the next step is to understand the functionality that the user needs to do the work. Using qualitative methods like interviews and focus groups, the usability evaluator gets a picture from the users of the functions that they want (i.e., the USER model). The third lens is the functionality that is actually used in performing the work, the ACTIVITY model. This functionality is identified by analyzing information collected through observation, shadowing, examining notes, reviewing training and procedural documents and similar ethnographic methods.[51]

Armed with information from the above three models—the functionality the system has, the functionality the user wants, and the functionality that is actually used—the TURF analysis can identify the overlap between the sets of functionality.[51] It is straightforward to determine how closely the existing system satisfies the users' wanted functionality and the functionality required to do the work. In addition to providing the usability evaluator with a list of gaps or deficiencies in the existing application against the other two lists, there are three measures of usefulness that can be identified from this information:

- How much of the functionality from the ontology is included in the functionality of the DESIGNER model:

$$\frac{[\text{Count of all functions in the ontology that are also in the DESIGNER model}]}{[\text{Count of all functions in the DESIGNER model}]}$$

- How much of the functionality from the ontology that is in all three models is included in the functionality of the DESIGNER model:

$$\frac{[\text{Count of all functions in the ontology that are also in any of the models}]}{[\text{Count of all functions in the DESIGNER model}]}$$

- How much of the functionality that is in all three models is provided by the functionality in the DESIGN model:

$$\frac{[\text{Count of all functions in the DESIGNER model}]}{[\text{Count of all functions in all of the models}]}$$

Combining the information realized from the ontology with the information from the models, the usability evaluator can also analyze the list to identify how the functionality identified in the ontology maps to the information from the models. That is, is there functionality from the ontology that is missing from the other models? Alternatively, do the models specify functionality that is not included in the ontology? If so, does the ontology need to be modified or is the specific functionality superfluous? This level of analysis provides the usability evaluator with exceptional insight into the ability of the system to meet the needs of the users in the completion of their work.

We had mentioned at the beginning of the discussion on functionality that there are three ways to analyze functionality. The ontology gives us an overarching view of the functional requirements from a domain view and the usefulness of the system can be analyzed using the functional models just discussed. The final way to explore functionality is based on a close examination of the user interface.

In this approach we look at the DESIGNER model of the system. A hierarchical model of the user interface is created by walking through the user interface and collecting screen captures. From the screenshots, each interface object is noted and cataloged. As part of this process, each item is categorized as an object or operation, where an operation is an interface item that can be used to cause an action to occur on the user interface. Objects, on the other hand, are inert; they may be used to organize items on the screen, like lines or symbols, or for general information, like a title or company logo. Operations are further classified as a domain function or an overhead function. The distinction is that domain functions are changing the inputs or otherwise advancing users toward completing their domain work. Overhead functions can, for example, help the user navigate through the application and do not contribute in a domain-specific way.[50]

With the user interface items now classified as objects or overhead operations or domain operations, the usability evaluator can provide several measures of usefulness by showing the number of domain operations versus the number of objects, and also by showing the number of domain operations versus the number of overhead operations. Figure 5-40 shows an interface with 24% objects and 76% operations, and that of the operations, 28% were overhead functions and the other 72% were domain functions. To improve the usability of the interface, examine the objects and the overhead functions to see if they can be eliminated or modified to streamline the user experience. The goal is to avoid distracting user interface objects and eliminate unnecessary overhead functions to enable the user to focus on domain-related functions.

TASK. TURF handles task analysis, utilizing methods that are discussed in this section, namely through the combined use of Goals-Operators-Methods-Selection (GOMS) rules and Keystroke Level Model (KLM). At the abstract level, these methods both take the general approach of breaking a task into its component activities and then using activity models to estimate the time and number of steps that will be required to complete the task. Looking at the details of both processes, there are differences in how the two processes reached their results. Once the task has been broken into the component tasks, either of the processes can be employed to estimate user performance. (CogTools (http://cogtool.hcii.cs.cmu.edu/) is a free software tool inspired by GOMS and offered by Carnegie Mellon that is highly regarded for estimating user performance.) The reader is referred to the respective sections for these methods for more details.

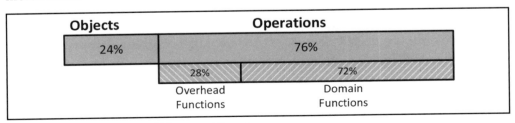

Figure 5-40: User Interface Objects and Functions

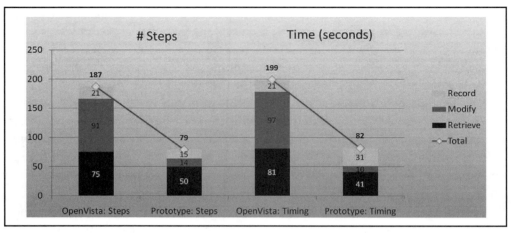

Figure 5-41: Improvement in Task Performance Following Redesign *(Reprinted from Journal of Biomedical Informatics, 44/6, Zhang J, Walji MF. Toward a unified framework of EHR usability, 1056-1067, 2011, with permission from Elsevier.)*

The key point is that when conducting the task analysis of an EHR using TURF, the results of GOMS and KLM can identify tasks that are disproportionate in the number of required steps or the amount of time they require from the user. These measures are valuable also when redesigning a performance issue, as they allow the developers to determine if there have been improvements. This is illustrated in Figure 5-41, which shows the impact of design changes on an EHR.

REPRESENTATION. A unique aspect of TURF is its incorporation of representation effects. This concept studies the effectiveness of information being displayed to the user. Because the presentation of information makes a profound impact on users, analyzing the representation of information can enable the usability evaluator to discover significant ways to improve an application, or to perform a comparison between similar applications.

Representations can be examined using different approaches. The first approach is to compare what is called the represent*ed* data against the represent*ing* data to ensure that there is a match.[66] The represented data are collected from the domain in the real world; the representing data are the way the information is displayed by the application. For example, cholesterol levels are typically reported as numbers, yet the information can be displayed by an application as numbers in a text box with color highlighting to show values that are out of the desired range, or as a series of historical numbers in a table with similar color highlighting, or as a graph showing trends in vital signs.

SCALE MATCHING. The main reason to understand represented data versus representing data is to ensure that the representing data are using the correct *scale* when displaying the information. *Scale* refers to the level of measurement used in statistics and research, and it relates to the types of operations that are valid for that type of scale. There are four levels of scale: nominal, ordinal, interval and ratio. On the low end, nominal variables are assigned values like animal, vegetable or mineral. It makes no sense to do math on nominal variables. At the high end, ratio variables have a true 0 (zero) and values can be compared mathematically. Speed is a good example, since we can have a speed of zero miles per hour; and, going 60 miles per hour is twice as fast as going 30 miles per hour.[67]

This becomes important because the scale of a variable influences how that variable should be displayed. We can count nominal variables, but it will cause eyebrows to furrow if one were to say, "My rose quartz crystal is twice as good as his pumpkin squash." This type of comparison is not valid with nominal variables (or with ordinal variables, where order can be determined). Even with ratio variables, it is possible to make comparisons that do not fit with their scale. Imagine getting a call from your physician's office after having your cholesterol tested and being told, "You got three scores." You would expect to get a value that would tell if your low-density lipoprotein (LDL) or high-density lipoprotein (HDL) or total were within acceptable ranges; knowing only the count of items that were measured would result in information being lost that could be important.

When the EHR is presenting information to users, the usability evaluator can identify the scale of the represented data and compare that to the scale of the representing data. Wherever mismatches occur, confusion may occur for the user or viewer of the information. (For more detailed coverage of the relationship between levels of measurement and dimensions, see Zhang's article, "A Representational Analysis of Relational Displays.")[67]

AFFORDANCES. The usability evaluator using the TURF framework should also explore the degree to which the application provides cues to the user, as opposed to requiring the user to rely on memory. These electronic breadcrumbs which users can follow are also referred to as *affordances.*[68] Some readers may remember the period when Microsoft Word® was a new application challenging WordPerfect® for dominance in the word processing arena. Word used simple-to-navigate menus, whereas WordPerfect required users to memorize keystrokes (or use a maddening plastic template that fit over the function keys). Expert WordPerfect users loved their powerful product and were able to work more quickly than Word users; however, new users loved the visible menu system and hated having to memorize keystroke combinations that were not intuitive when they faced a much shorter learning curve with Word. The rest is history: to this day, Word is the dominant word-processing application because it did a much better job of making the application usable for new users.

To evaluate how well an application succeeds at presenting affordances, Zhang and Walji used expert review. Independent reviewers worked through different scenarios and indicated whether the application presented cues that served as high, medium or low levels of affordance. A high percentage of high affordance is regarded as an indicator of a well-designed user interface. Conversely, an application with lower levels of affordance presents opportunities to improve user cues.[51]

HEURISTIC EVALUATION. The third method that TURF utilizes to evaluate representation is the use of heuristic evaluations. Heuristic evaluation has been discussed previously and the approach utilized by TURF is the same as the previously discussed process. Here, we will note six of the heuristic principles that are especially relevant to the representation analysis: Consistency, Visibility, Match, Minimalist, Memory and Feedback. When doing a heuristic evaluation, the findings for these principles will enable the designers and developers to learn about any violations of heuristic principles. These can lead to changes that will improve the user interface.[51]

Conducting a Heuristic Evaluation

Participants: The TURF framework for evaluating usability is a collection of methods that can be done serially or in parallel. The availability of both tangible and financial resources will determine how many people can be used to conduct a usability evaluation using the TURF framework.

- Five testers are recommended for the heuristic evaluation.
- The functional analysis and representation methods that use expert review should have at least two reviewers.
- While a single person can conduct many of the different evaluation methods, a TURF framework evaluation is benefitted if it is led by experienced usability evaluators.

Materials:

- Pencil and paper or electronic recording devices for the interviewing sessions
- Pencil and paper or suitable software for recording task analysis and representation activities
- Optional ontology software for the ontology development
- Diagramming software for producing the ontology diagram (in the absence of graphical ontology software)

Process:

Because TURF is such an encompassing framework, we will focus on high-level activities for this part of the TURF description.

1. The most important part of the TURF methodology is to identify the stakeholders and where the application is in its lifecycle.
   a. If the application is in the early stages of architecture and design, user analysis is critical, as understanding the user characteristics and needs will guide future decisions.
   b. A common mistake is to overlook ancillary users—those who are not physicians, physician assistants (PAs), nurse practitioners (NPs), or nurses—when deciding who needs to be involved in user interface design.
   c. Ask stakeholders for a commitment of their time to participate in the activities. For those who have heavy demands on their time, tell them up front how much time it will take and how often they need to contribute. Be prepared to do some negotiating!
2. A useful question to ask during the initial stages is, "What must happen that will tell you that this effort has been a success?" You are looking for an answer that describes some type of observable or measurable activity or achievement.
3. Develop a plan to conduct the evaluation, including who needs to participate and how long they will need to participate. Risk factors to consider:
   a. Experience of the usability evaluators
   b. Availability of participants (just scheduling meetings for people in demand can take much longer than one would anticipate)

  c. Necessary resources, in addition to people

   i. Access to computers and the target application

   ii. Room for the evaluation

   iii. Recording equipment, if available

4. Keep stakeholders, especially participants, regularly informed of progress and any changes to scheduled activities. Keeping people informed is essential to sustaining interest and enthusiasm.

5. After activities have been completed, ensure that participants and stakeholders know when findings or other information will be available. Provide updates until the evaluation is finalized.

6. Recognize all participants and stakeholders for their role in the evaluation project.

Variations:

- Time and resource constraints can dictate that certain methods are deferred or skipped.

Example. Figure 5-42 is from an evaluation utilizing the TURF framework of the military's EHR, the Armed Forces Health Longitudinal Technology Application (AHLTA). The evaluation was performed by Zhang, Walji, Patel, Gimble and Zhang in 2009. This evaluation provides some excellent examples of the products of the TURF functional analysis. (Note that TURF was called UFuRT when this study was performed.)[69]

The initial effort was to create a system hierarchy. This was accomplished by going through all screens of the application and documenting every interface item (text labels, fields for entering data, menus, icons, etc.). This information was visualized using Protégé, an open-source ontology tool (http://protege.stanford.edu). Following is the visualization of the top three levels of the resulting hierarchy.[69]

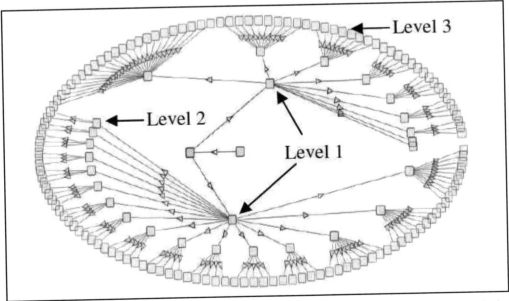

Figure 5-42: Visualization of Top Three Functional Levels of AHLTA *(Reprinted from Journal of Biomedical Informatics, 44/6, Zhang J, Walji MF. Toward a unified framework of EHR usability, 1056-1067, 2011, with permission from Elsevier.)*

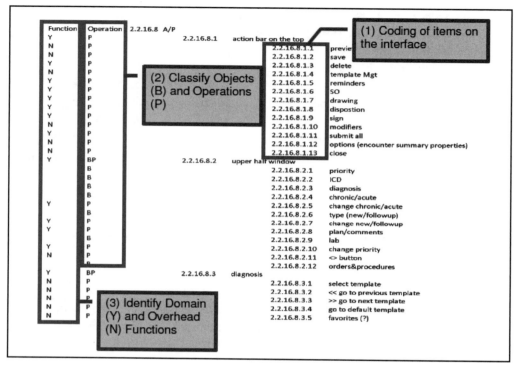

Figure 5-43: Classifying User Interface Items *(Reprinted from Journal of Biomedical Informatics, 44/6, Zhang J, Walji MF. Toward a unified framework of EHR usability, 1056-1067, 2011, with permission from Elsevier.)*

After compiling the list of interface items, expert review was used to categorize each of the items in the hierarchy as an object or an operation. As was discussed in the TURF Description section previously presented, an object is an inert user interface item and an operation is a user interface item that can cause a change to the user interface or cause an action to occur in the application. Once the objects and operations had been identified, the operation items were then classified as either domain items or overhead items. Domain items are distinguished, as their operations contribute to completing the work, whereas overhead objects are more likely to handle duties like navigation or formatting. Figure 5-43 illustrates how the items are documented and how they are classified as objects or operations.[69]

With the identification of objects, domain functions and overhead functions, it was a small step to produce charts that illustrate the findings of the functional analysis (Figure 5-44). The first of these was two pie charts. One of the pie charts shows the percentage of user interface objects that are objects or operations, and the other pie chart shows the percentages of the operations from the first pie chart that are domain functions or overhead functions.[69]

The system view is interesting, but more information is provided by examining the breakout by functional area. Figure 5-45 shows how functional areas compared against each other.[69]

The chart (Figure 5-45) shows the disparity between functional areas in the ratio of domain functions to overhead functions. A high percentage of overhead functions represents an area of the application to focus on to improve usability by streamlining the screens with a large number of overhead functions.

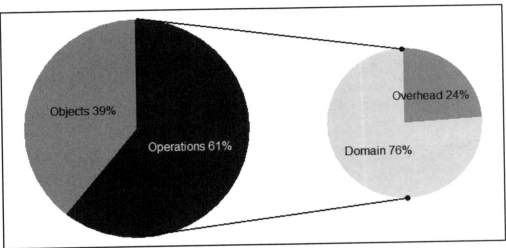

Figure 5-44: Interface Items: Objects & Operations; Overhead & Domain Operations *(Reprinted from Journal of Biomedical Informatics, 44/6, Zhang J, Walji MF. Toward a unified framework of EHR usability, 1056-1067, 2011, with permission from Elsevier.)*

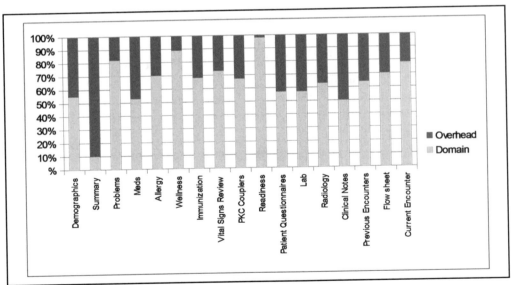

Figure 5-45: Operation Types by Functional Area *(Reprinted from Journal of Biomedical Informatics, 44/6, Zhang J, Walji MF. Toward a unified framework of EHR usability, 1056-1067, 2011, with permission from Elsevier.)*

☺	Comprehensive usability framework utilizing multiple usability activities
☺	Can be used throughout lifecycle, from design through sustaining activities
☺	Many incorporated methods provide quantitative feedback
☺	Provides tangible feedback for improving usability
☺	Components of framework can be used individually to target areas of interest
☺	TURF software tool developed to simplify evaluations
☹	Not advised for inexperienced usability specialists
☹	Requires solid planning and communication to execute full-blown evaluation
☹	Ontology development requires unique skills

Figure 5-46: Pros and Cons of TURF

Summary. The TURF framework gives the usability evaluator a level of usability information that cannot be matched. The framework utilizes a diverse set of methods to inspect and analyze an application. Given the risks associated with poor usability of an EHR and the benefits of an application that users want to use, an evaluation using the TURF framework will point out deficiencies in an existing design and provide ideas for how to enhance the usability of the EHR. Additionally, TURF utilizes numerous methods that allow the usability evaluator to quantify the usability of an EHR, which makes the findings more credible than subjective assessments. Finally, as an alternative to a costly hardware usability lab,[58] there is now a TURF software tool that simplifies conducting a usability analysis using the TURF framework. The tool is currently available at https://turf.shis.uth.tmc.edu/turfweb/index.asp as a free download. The TURF framework is the gold standard for usability specialists, EHR vendors and EHR users who want to see their application reach the pinnacle of usability. Figure 5-46 points out the pros and cons of using TURF.

CONCLUSION

This chapter has provided several usability evaluation methods, ranging from simple to difficult in complexity and ease of use. Each tool provides different information, making it important to use a complement of tools to capture key information and maximize usability. The next chapter describes building a business case in order to obtain approval and resources for improving usability from planning and design to post-implementation optimization.

REFERENCES

1. Tague NR. Affinity Diagram. *ASQ*. 2004. Available at: http://asq.org/learn-about-quality/idea-creation-tools/overview/affinity.html. Accessed June 24, 2013.

2. Rettger MB. The seven habits of highly effective usability people. *Journal of Usability Studies*. May 2010; 5(3):76-80.

3. Igarcia. The Affinity Diagram Tool. *Six Sigma Daily*. December 25, 2012. Available at: http://www.sixsigmadaily.com/methodology/the-affinity-diagram-tool. Accessed June 24, 2013.

4. Seneler CO, Basoglu N, Daim TU. A Taxonomy for Technology Adoption: A Human Computer Interaction Perspective. *PICMET 2008 Proceedings*. July 2008:2208-1219.

5. Wilson C. *User Experience Re-Mastered: Your Guide to Getting the Right Design*. Burlington, MA: Morgan Kaufmann, 2010.

6. Glassdoor.com. G2 USA. *Glassdoor.com*. Oct 10, 2011. Available at: http://www.glassdoor.com/Photos/G2-USA-Office-Photos-E28868.htm. Accessed June 28, 2013.

7. Usability Guidelines. *Usability.Gov*. 2006. Available at: http://www.usability.gov/guidelines/guidelines_book.pdf. Accessed June 28, 2013.

8. Hudson W. Card Sorting. In: Soegaard M, Dam RF, eds. *Interaction Design Foundation*. 2013. Available at: http://www.interaction-design.org/encyclopedia/card_sorting.html. Accessed June 29, 2013.

9. Maat HP, Lentz L. Using Sorting Data to Evaluate Text Structure: An Evidence-based Proposal for Restructuring Patient Information Leaflets. *Technical Communications*. August 2011; 58(3):197-216.

10. Knight K. Usability Testing with Card Sorting. *Six Revisions*. April 25, 2011. Available at: http://sixrevisions.com/usabilityaccessibility/card-sorting/. Accessed June 30, 2013.

11. Card Sorting: How Many Users to Test. *Nielsen Norman Group*. July 19, 2004. Available at: http://www.nngroup.com/articles/card-sorting-how-many-users-to-test/. Accessed June 29, 2013.

12. Pierotti D. Usability Techniques: Heuristic Evaluation, a System Checklist. *Society for Technical Communications*. 1995. Available at: http://www.stcsig.org/usability/topics/articles/he-checklist.html. Accessed May 15, 2012.

13. Vankipuram M, Kahol K, Cohen T, et al. Toward automated workflow analysis and visualization in clinical environments. *J Biomed Inform*. June 2011; 44(3):434-440.

14. Zheng K, Haftel HM, Hirschl RB, et al. Quantifying the impact of health IT implementations on clinical workflow: a new methodological perspective. *J Am Med Assoc*. September 2010; 17(5):454-461.

15. Drazen E. *Using Tracking Tools to Improve Patient Flow in Hospitals*. Oakland: California HealthCare Foundation, 2011.

16. Ling S, Schmidt H. Time Petri Nets for Workflow Modelling and Analysis. *Proceedings of the IEEE International Conference on Systems, Man and Cybernetics*. 2000; 4:3039-3044.

17. Kushinka SA. *Workflow Analysis: EHR Deployment Techniques*. Oakland, CA: California HealthCare Foundation, 2011.

18. DOQ-IT. *A Systems Approach to Operational Redesign – Workbook*: MassPro, 2006.

19. HIMSS. *Workflow Redesign in Support of Use of Information Technology Within Healthcare: A HIMSS Toolkit*. Chicago, IL: Healthcare Information and Management Systems Society (HIMSS), 2010.

20. Aarts J, Ash J, Berg M. Extending the understanding of computerized physician order entry: Implications for professional collaboration, workflow and quality of care. *Int J Med Inform*. 2007; 76(Supplement 1):S4-S13.

21. Corrao NJ, Robinson AG, Swiernik MA, et al. Importance of Testing for Usability When Selecting and Implementing an Electronic Health or Medical Record System. *J Onc Pract*. May 2010; 6(3):120-124.

22. Verdon DR. EHR Divorce: What's Driving Dissatisfaction. *Med Econ*. June 2013; 23-27.

23. Ault A. Survey says doctors' dissatisfaction with EHRs is rising. *Health Reference Center - Academic.* April 1, 2013. Available at: http://go.galegroup.com/ps/i.do?id=GALE%7CA328165035&v=2.1&u=tx-shracd2509&it=r&p=HRCA&sw=w&asid=52c39d2dbff0b3aa863a6d93b601c4e7. Accessed July 24, 2013.

24. Campbell EM, Guappone KP, Sittig DF, et al. Computerized provider order entry adoption: implications for clinical workflow. *J Gen Intern Med.* November 2008; 24(1):21-26.

25. Kushniruk A, Borycki E, Kuwata S, et al. Predicting Changes in Workflow Resulting from Healthcare Information Systems: Ensuring the Safety of Healthcare. *Healthc Q.* October 2006; 9(Special Issues):114-118.

26. Brannon N, Koubek R, Havey C. *Usability Analysis.* Dayton, OH and Norman, OK: Wright State University and University of Oklahoma, 1999.

27. Johnson C, Johnston D, Crowley PK, et al. *EHR Usability Toolkit: A Background Report on Usability and Electronic Health Records (Prepared by Westat under Contract No. HHSA 290-2009-00023I).* Rockville, MD: Agency for Healthcare Research and Quality (AHRQ); August 2011.

28. Karahoca A, Bayraktar E, Tatoglu E, et al. Infromation system design for a hospital emergency department: A usability analysis of software prototypes. *J Biomed Inform.* April 2010; 43(2):224-232.

29. Shneiderman B, Plaisant C. *Designing the User Interface: Strategies for Effective Human-Computer Interaction.* 5th ed. Boston, MA: Addison Wesley, 2010.

30. Kushniruk AW, Patel VL. Cognitive and usability engineering methods for the evaluation of clinical information systems. *J Biomed Inform.* February 2004; 37(1):56-76.

31. Wikipedia contributors. GOMS. *Wikipedia, The Free Encyclopedia.* August 7, 2013. Available at: http://en.wikipedia.org/w/index.php?title=GOMS&oldid=567549708. Accessed August 17, 2013.

32. Nielsen J, Mack RL. *Usability Inspection Methods.* New York: John Wiley & Sons, Inc., 1993.

33. Nielsen J. 10 Usability Heuristics for User Interface Design. In Nielsen J, ed. *NN/g Nielsen Norman Group.* January 1, 1995. Available at: http://www.nngroup.com/articles/ten-usability-heuristics/. Accessed August 18, 2013.

34. Shneiderman B. Designing for fun: how can we design user interfaces to be more fun? *Interactions.* Sept-Oct 2004; 11(5):48-50.

35. Connell IW. *Full Principles Set.* London: University College London Interaction Centre, 2000.

36. Gerhardt-Powals J. Cognitive engineering principles for enhancing human–computer performance. *Int J Hum Comput interact.* 1996; 8(2).

37. Heuristic evaluation. *Wikipedia, The Free Encyclopedia.* August 10, 2013. Available at: http://en.wikipedia.org/w/index.php?title=Heuristic_evaluation&oldid=567983677. Accessed August 19, 2013.

38. First Principles of Interaction Design. *AskTog.com.* 2003. Available at: http://www.asktog.com/basics/firstPrinciples.html. Accessed August 19, 2013.

39. Zhang J, Johnson TR, Patel VL, et al. Using usability heuristics to evaluate patient safety of medical devices. *J Biomed Inform.* 2003; 36(1):23-30.

40. How many test users in a usability study? *NN/g Nielsen Norman Group.* June 4, 2012. Available at: http://www.nngroup.com/articles/how-many-test-users/. Accessed August 18, 2013.

41. US Department of Veterans Affairs National Center for Patient Safety. Basics of Healthcare Failure Mode Effect and Analysis; Ann Arbor, MI; 2005. Available at: http://www.patientsafety.va.org/SafetyTopics/HFMEA/FMEA2.pdf.

42. Stalhandske E, DeSosier J, Wilson R, et al. Healthcare FMEA in the Veterans Health Administration. In Carr S, ed. *Patient Safety and Quality Healthcare.* September 2009. Available at: http://www.psqh.com/septemberoctober-2009/239-healthcare-fmea-in-the-veterans-health-administration.html. Accessed August 23, 2013.

43. Cohen M. *Medication Errors*. Washington, DC: American Pharmacists Association, 2007.

44. VA National Center for Patient Safety. *The Basics of Healthcare Failure Mode and Effect Analysis*. VA National Center for Patient Safety; 2002.

45. Card SK, Moran TP, Newell A. The Keystroke-Level Model for User Performance Time with Interactive Systems. *Communications of the ACM*. July 2000; 23(7):396-410.

46. Kieras D. *Using the Keystroke-Level Model to Estimate Execution Time*: University of Michigan, 2001.

47. Saitwal H, Feng X, Walji M, et al. Assessing the performance of an Electronic Health Record (EHR) using Cognitive Task Analysis. *Int J Med Inform*. July 2010; 79(7):501-506.

48. Hayes BE. *Measuring Customer Satisfaction: Survey Design, Use, and Statistical Analysis of Methods*. 2nd ed. Milwaukee, WI: ASQ Quality Press, 1998.

49. Tullis T, Albert B. *Measuring the User Experience*. Boston: Morgan Kaufmann, 2008.

50. Lewis JR. IBM Computer usability satisfaction questionnaires: Psychometric evaluation and instructions for use. *Int J Hum Comput Interact*. 1995; 7(1):57-78.

51. Zhang J, Walji MF. TURF: Toward a unified framework of EHR usability. *J Biomed Inform*. December 2011; 44(6):1056-1067.

52. Patel VL, Arocha JF, Kaufman DR. A Primer on Aspects of Cognition for Medical Informatics. *J Am Med Inform Assoc*. July 2001; 8(4):324-343.

53. Zhang J, Patel VL, Johnson TR, et al. *Evaluating and Predicting Patient Safety for Medical Devices with Integral Information Technology*. Rockville, MD: Agency for Healthcare Research and Quality, 2005. PMID: 21249841.

54. Nielsen J. *Usability Engineering*. Boston: Morgan Kaufmann, 1993.

55. Rubin J, Chisnell D. *Handbook of Usability Testing: How to Plan, Design, and Conduct Effective Tests*. 2nd ed. Indianapolis, IN: Wiley Publishing, 2008.

56. Molich R. A Critique of "How To Specify the Participant Group Size for Usability Studies: A Practitioner's Guide" by Macefield. *Journal of Usability Studies*. May 2010; 5(3):124-128.

57. Kolko J. *Think Aloud User Testing*. Austin, TX. Austin College of Design, 2012. Available at http://www.ac4d.com/classes/201_open/03.AC4D_IDSE201_ThinkAloudProtocol.pdf.

58. Russ AL, Weiner M, Russell SA, et al. Design and Implementation of a Hospital-Based Usability Laboratory: Insights from a Department of Veterans Affairs Laboratory for Health Information Technology. *The Joint Commission Journal on Quality and Patient Safety*. December 2012; 38(12):531-540.

59. Segall N, Saville JG, L'Engle P, et al. Usability Evaluation of a Personal Health Record. Paper presented at: AMIA Annual Symposium Proceedings 2011; October 22, 2011; Washington, DC.

60. Why you only need to test with 5 users. *NN/g Nielsen Norman Group*. March 19, 2000. Available at: http://www.nngroup.com/articles/why-you-only-need-to-test-with-5-users/. Accessed June 20, 2013.

61. Li AC, Kannrya JL, Kushniruk A, et al. Integrating usability testing and think-aloud protocol analysis with "near-live" clinical simulations in evaluating clinical decision support. *Int J Med Inform*. 2012; 81:761-772.

62. Zhang J, Butler KA. UFuRT: A Work-Centered Framework and Process for Design and Evaluation of Information Systems. Proceedings of HCI International 2007, 2007.

63. Setback for Sutter after $1B EHR crashes. *Healthcare IT News*. August 28, 2013. Available at: http://www.healthcareitnews.com/news/setback-sutter-after-1b-ehr-system%20crashes. Accessed September 3, 2013.

64. The costly darkside of EMR implementation. *HIT Consultant*. January 3, 2013. Available at: http://www.hitconsultant.net/2013/01/03/the-costly-darkside-of-emr-implementations/. Accessed September 2, 2013.

65. Riaño D, Real F, López-Vallverdú JA, et al. An ontology-based personalization of health-care knowledge to support clinical decisions for chronically ill patients. *J Biomed Inform.* June 2012; 45(3):239-446.

66. Gong Y, Zhang J. Toward a human-centered hyperlipidemia management system: The interaction between internal and external information on relational data search. *J Med Sys.* May 2011; 35(2):169-177.

67. Zhang J. A Representation Analysis of Relational Displays. *Int J Hum Comput Stud.* 1996; 45:59-74.

68. Norman DA. *The Design of Everyday Things.* 2002 ed. Basic Books, 2002.

69. Zhang Z, Walji MF, Patel VL, et al. Functional Analysis of Interfaces in U.S. Military Electronic Health Record System using UFuRT Framework. Paper presented at: AMIA Annual Symposium 2009, 2009; Washington, DC.

CHAPTER 6

Building a Business Case for EHR Usability

"In order to realize the cost effectiveness of usability activities, you will need to move from an emergency room model to a wellness program."
—Susan Weinschenk[1]

Most healthcare professionals will readily appreciate the analogy of usability to emergency department care versus wellness care. It is much more expensive to treat patients in the emergency department when their disease has progressed and is more complicated and where wellness strategies of prevention and early intervention may be inappropriate and difficult to employ. Similarly, it is much more expensive to fix EHR usability issues following go-live than it is to employ a sound usability strategy throughout the product lifecycle from the beginning.

Two anecdotal quotes that signal an emergency department approach to usability include the following:

> *"Let's just get the EHR implemented and then we can fix things."*
> *"Usability is a distraction."*

Both are recent quotes from executives of two different healthcare systems, using two different EHRs. Not only do these kinds of messages send a distressing message to designers and developers who are passionate about creating products that their users will love—they also show that these executives fail to understand the costs and risks associated with "fixing things" after EHR go live. Specifically, they fail to understand the amount of resources employed for expensive emergency care versus those used in wellness care. Without a solid appreciation for the benefits of usability, how could they be expected to incorporate usability analyses into the evaluation of potential EHRs for their organization? Consequently, they may choose an EHR that has great features on paper but is a nightmare to deploy and frustrating for users. Equally disconcerting, they may be chasing Meaningful Use dollars, not realizing that those dollars, and then some, will be lost, and when they have to halt the implementation so they can "fix things."

As we go to press with this book, there are a lot of dissatisfied providers changing EHR systems.[2] As a matter of fact, 2013 is being touted as the year of EHR dissatisfaction with a record number of providers switching systems. Therefore, the ability to produce a compelling usability business case is not only timely but an essential tool that supports improved decision making.

CASE STUDY

One of the oft-cited business cases for usability is from McAfee, developer of antivirus software.[3] The introduction of McAfee's new ProtectionPlus software was followed by 20,000 downloads over a 10-week period but only 170 support line calls. This was approximately one-tenth the typical volume and about a third of the 170 calls were pre-sales questions and not support issues.

The low support needs were not a fluke and not by accident. The results followed a well-planned strategy by McAfee to make the user interface a priority. They began focusing on usability early in the product lifecycle, before the programming began in the architecture and design phases.

> *"Rather than shooting a whole movie and showing it to people to see if they like it, we put together a storyboard. That prototyping was very, very important."*[3]

McAfee employed an iterative design process that engaged users early on in product development.[3] By involving end users early in the process, they were able to focus on users' tasks, as opposed to application features. A product that worked the way users wanted helped them avoid the costs and efforts related to unnecessary features. But the bigger payoff of creating a simpler and easier-to-use product is the dramatically fewer number of dissatisfied users. Their usability efforts were rewarded with fewer support calls and associated costs following product release.

FINANCIAL IMPACT ANALYSES

The journey to a sound business case for EHR usability begins with an understanding of the different types of financial impact analyses that can be employed. Some of the more popular models are described next. In order to make sense of these, we will first discuss the core concept of "cost of change" to build a foundation for the discussions of the models.

Cost of Change Curve. This is a graphical representation of the increase in software-related *costs* (vertical axis) over *time* (x axis). The concept is derived from Boehm's hallmark 1976 work illustrating the relative cost to fix an error based on the software phase, represented as the point in the development lifecycle in which the error was corrected.[4] Boehm's work documented that the cost of changing software increases exponentially over time.

The concept of the cost of change curve in its simplest form is depicted in Figure 6-1. Newer methods for software development were intended to flatten the cost of change curve. However, this has not proved to be true in large software projects.[5]

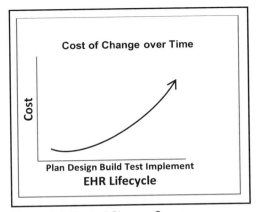

Figure 6-1: Cost of Change Curve

It is easy to appreciate that appropriate changes made early in the EHR lifecycle prevent costs associated with changes that occur later. Usability addressed early in development prevents costs associated with technical support, redesigning, reprogramming, retesting and retraining required if left until after go live. This explains how the analogy of emergency care versus wellness care equates with usability.[1] Usability addressed early on is easier and less costly, while later interventions to correct usability flaws are more difficult and costly.

In another EHR implementation, a list of items in the EHR was deemed too long and unwieldy for users. Keep in mind that costs had already been incurred at least once in designing the list, writing code for the list, testing the list and training people on the list. There are typically lots of lists in EHRs; too often they are based on individual impressions without the benefit of clinician input. In the absence of informed guidance, users end up having to wade through these long lists, hoping to find what they need without having to start over at the top. Clearly, this slows user productivity and is another cost incurred. To improve this situation, items not used on the list can be removed to improve usability and thus user productivity. However, additional costs will now be incurred to redesign, reprogram, retest and retrain users. It would have been less expensive had usability testing been employed earlier in the lifecycle to detect these types of problems. Said differently, prevention, like wellness care, would have been the best strategy.

A recent report by KLAS highlighted the current reality of the cost of change curve for usability. The author, Mark Wagner, is quoted as saying, "The financial investment in EMR technology can be large for providers, but this investment pales in comparison to the outlay in effort providers are making to customize the products to achieve high usability."[6] No doubt there are opportunities for improvement in usability prior to EHR acquisition that would decrease the costs buyers are incurring to make the EHRs more usable, useful and satisfactory.

Total Cost of Ownership (TCO). TCO analyses focus on costs relative to the lifetime of the EHR project. It includes not only the initial acquisition costs but also ongoing support costs, upgrade fees and other longer-term costs.[7] TCO can vary by as much as 200 percent, depending on the EHR brand.[7]

TCO analysis is very important for buyers when considering EHR purchases. High upfront costs may be repellant to potential buyers when compared to competitive EHRs with lower entry costs. However, lower long-term costs can make EHRs with higher sticker prices more attractive by offsetting the entry cost when the year-over-year costs are considered. *Caveat emptor;* buyer beware.

While usability can be a major factor in TCO, it is rarely considered when purchasing.[8] Buyers usually do not have an understanding of EHR product usability and related costs, as EHR vendors rarely provide information on the subject. What buyers will see, however, when they have an EHR with poor usability, either due to out-of-box deficiencies or because the buyer has made changes to the EHR that negatively impact usability, is an unexpected increase in overhead costs caused by time-consuming, error-prone and difficult to use EHRs.[8]

Return on Investment (ROI). This is a measure of financial performance expressed as the ratio of profit or loss relative to the cost of achieving it. ROI may yield the most powerful value proposition for improving EHR usability because it provides a financial metric that illustrates the financial impact to the bottom line.[9] ROI quantifies the upfront investment for usability over the lifetime of the product, recognizing that early efforts to detect and improve usability are cheaper than redesign later in the development cycle.[10]

ROI can be viewed in three different ways: internal, external and social.[11] *Internal ROI* refers to the perceived or actual efficiencies that occur during product development related to usability improvement efforts such as decreased development and maintenance costs. *External ROI* focuses on improved profitability that can be attributed to improved usability such as improved customer retention, reduced support calls and enhanced brand awareness. *Social ROI* is about the perceptions of internal stakeholders, such as managers and developers, that usability does impact ROI by improving the value of the product.

Examining ROI through these different lenses is important in seeing the whole picture. Not doing so is analogous to measuring weight without height, which is difficult to interpret and act upon. Understanding all three types of ROI provides a clearer meaning of ROI and illuminates the direction to take. For example, social ROI can affect both internal and external ROI, making it an important measure. If internal ROI is insufficient, the appropriate strategy may be in improving social ROI.

ROI should be expressed in the business case as increases or decreases over a year. Annualized dollars are consistent with other financial tools used by decision makers, specifically those in management and finance. For example, if it is expected that improvement in usability will decrease the cost to train end users by 25%, and current costs are estimated to be 1,000 employees a year at $100 an hour for 12 hours, savings would be reported as $300,000 annually.

Cost-Benefit Analysis (CBA). The idea that the cost of usability exceeds the benefit is outdated.[12] Like most things, it depends on how well usability is applied, meaning how effectively usability is incorporated into the EHR lifecycle and how efficiently the work is performed. Better stated, "Ease of use doesn't come from wishful thinking. It comes from conducting systematic usability engineering activities throughout the project lifecycle. This is real work and costs real money, though not as much as some people fear."[13]

CBA, expressed as a cost-benefit ratio, is an ROI tool for quantifying the predicted costs and benefits. It can be used to demonstrate the impact of good usability in EHRs during the initial development. Alternatively, CBA can also be used to demonstrate costs and benefits of improving the usability from the current state of an EHR to the future state of the EHR.

The costs of better usability can be viewed in four categories: one-time costs, recurring costs, redesign costs and cost savings. One-time costs, also known as upfront costs, may involve initial costs such as specialized training or creating a usability lab for evaluation.[14] Recurring costs can be salary or consulting costs for professionals involved in the usability evaluation.[14] Redesign costs are incurred if and when redesign is required based on the findings of the usability evaluation.[14] Cost savings (or cost avoidance) can be measured by comparing the costs of current or poor usability with the savings achieved by good usability, such as costs saved in productivity, training and support.

When predicting costs in the business case, there are different types of costs to consider, including direct and indirect, fixed and variable. Direct costs are costs that can be specifically tied to the usability project. These typically include salaries, wages and benefits of employees involved in the project, as well as travel, equipment, materials and supplies. Direct costs for usability testing may also include costs for usability experts, testing, recruiting and using subject matter experts, training, and consulting services.

Indirect costs are costs not directly attributable to the usability project. They are costs absorbed by a number of projects and can include equipment, materials or supplies used over multiple projects, including computers, paper and pens, or utilities, rent, phone services and security. Indirect costs can be fixed or variable. Fixed costs are those that do not vary over time such as overhead costs including building rent or mortgage. As the name implies, variable costs will vary over time. Fixed costs plus variable costs yield total costs of the project.

The inclusion of accurate and appropriate costs in the business case is important, demonstrating a comprehensive analysis and anticipation of potential questions by key stakeholders. The primary audience of the business case will be management, which is expecting a sound, convincing financial case.[15] Next we will examine the benefits of good usability.

VENDOR PERSPECTIVE

Software vendors considering the inclusion of usability testing in their product lifecycle will undoubtedly want to know the costs and benefits in order to justify the effort.[13] Lack of knowledge of the benefits of usability may explain in part the insufficient focus on usability in EHR product development. Several significant benefits warrant the inclusion of usability in the EHR lifecycle.

Reduction in Development Costs. Usability testing during the lifecycle helps reduce development costs by producing a product that has only relevant functionality[16] and good workflow. Costs are also reduced by detecting and correcting usability problems early in the development process and avoiding costlier fixes later in the lifecycle.[16] Together, these can create a shortened development time that reduces costs by spending less on human resources and overhead.[1]

Reduction in Documentation Costs. With better EHR usability, users will rely less on documentation materials such as user manuals.[9] The decreased need for documentation results in diminished costs associated with development and printing. Having less to document reduces the need for user manuals, as the interface is far more intuitive.[17]

Reduction in Support Costs. With good usability, there are fewer user support needs and associated costs.[9] When users find the EHR usable, useful and satisfying, they are able to learn the application more quickly and are less likely to need support during and after implementation.[9]

Reduction in Maintenance Costs. Using usability to better target design can result in fewer design iterations.[1] Vendors will avoid spending money that would otherwise be spent on correcting issues that annoyed users as reported following implementation.[9]

Increased Customer Satisfaction and Retention. Good usability leads to satisfied customers who are unlikely to look for a replacement EHR. While this is a very important benefit, this can be difficult to measure.

Enhanced Marketability. Good usability that is readily demonstrated to potential buyers can result in a competitive advantage.[16] The result is a lower cost to sell and improved customer loyalty with attendant benefits to revenue. Donald Norman describes usability as "the next competitive frontier," differentiating one software application from another in the marketplace.[18]

There is no magic formula for estimating the financial impact of usability on an EHR vendor's business. Multiple variables can influence the outcome such as business strategy, organizational culture, EHR product's current state of usability, the state of usability in competitors' products and more. Maximizing the benefit requires knowledgeable usability experts to guide and evaluate the process and ensure the best outcomes. Where you must estimate costs, resources or timelines, state your assumptions and be prepared to defend them.

BUYER PERSPECTIVE

Vendors are not alone in tackling usability. Buyers who customize "out-of-the-box" EHRs become involved in usability, especially when they customize the user interface to meet their unique needs.[19] Having adequate resources to appropriately incorporate usability in the EHR is imperative; otherwise buyers will find themselves on the wrong side of the cost of change curve. Therefore, it is important for buyers to understand usability and the implications to their organizations, both in benefits and costs.

Reduction in Training Costs. Buyers can achieve excellent savings with good usability, as an improved user interface makes the EHR easier to learn; acquired operational knowledge is easier to retain, thereby requiring less retraining when mobile users must master multiple EHRs.[9,16] Tied in with this benefit is faster onboarding of new employees, temporary or PRN staff such as *locum tenens*, consultants, students, interns and residents.

Reduction in Support Costs. Not only is learning faster, but retention of operational knowledge is greater, thereby enabling users to perform their duties efficiently without the need for disruptive technical support requests.[16] With good usability, buyers should see improved savings as fewer support specialists will be required to handle the reduced number of calls. A related benefit is that when support is requested, the time to resolve a problem should be reduced, too.[16]

Reduction in Adoption Costs. Usability is a key factor in EHR adoption.[20] EHRs that are intuitive to learn and deemed usable and useful by users are more readily adopted, thereby saving buyers in adoption costs, such as additional training and end-user support for poor usability EHRs. Another aspect of this issue is that poor adoption is a driving factor in healthcare facilities that are replacing EHRs. "Time is money" to providers, which, when translated to applications that are burdensome to use, means forcing physicians to spend time in the EHR reduces the time they can spend on revenue-generating activities.

Reduction in Customization Costs. EHR buyers can dramatically reduce costs of customization by employing good usability early in the lifecycle prior to implementation. This will help reduce costs associated with poor usability and fixes post-implementation,[16] as well as costs associated with a prolonged customization process such as costly software designers, developers, testers, trainers and technical writers.[1]

Increased User Satisfaction. End-user satisfaction is a factor in EHR adoption and use. Additionally usable and useful EHRs create satisfied users. While there are several tools to measure user satisfaction with EHRs, illustrating the value proposition can be challenging. Perhaps the cases of physician dissatisfaction leading to revolts against unwanted EHRs can be used to highlight the risk of inflaming the physician community and the loss of goodwill.

Increased User Productivity. Better EHR usability results in improved task time, greater efficiency and increased user productivity, thereby saving time and money.[16,21] The ability to improve productivity through improved usability has been empirically demonstrated.[22]

Decreased Use Errors. Good EHR usability improves user learning and navigation, thereby decreasing chances of error. "Even better than good error messages is a careful design, which prevents a problem from occurring in the first place."[23]

Hospitals can have hundreds of costly software applications in production at any one time, making the thought of usability evaluation overwhelming. Even a basic EHR application in a physician practice can prove challenging when there are limited resources. The key is to understand the implications of EHR usability as it relates to costs and benefits. EHR buyers are unfortunately being incentivized by Meaningful Use dollars to implement EHRs without sufficient consideration to usability. It is too easy to get caught in the trap of trying to make the best of a multimillion dollar purchase only to find yourself on the wrong side of usability and the cost of change curve.

> *"A focus on short-term cost considerations, as a main driving force in procuring new information technology, always comes with a hefty price down the road, a price that always weighs most heavily on users' shoulders."*[24]

BUSINESS CASE TEMPLATE

Business cases are tools that can be used for proposing a usability evaluation. It should provide clear justification for undertaking usability testing and include a method for demonstrating financial impact as well as benefits. The key to creating a successful business case is to be concise and yet comprehensive, focusing on essential information to create an informed decision by readers. The steps for developing a business case are described next.

Executive Summary. The first part of the business case provides a summary of the essential elements intended to capture and sustain readers' interest. It should include the business need, proposed solution, high-level benefits of solution, serious risks and time frame for completion. Stylistically, this section should favor conciseness and clarity. This section is typically written last to capture the essence of the business case that is provided in more detail in later sections.

Business Need. This section details the business need driving the usability project. Specific questions to answer include the following:

- What is the problem the organization is trying to fix or the opportunity to capture, and what impact is it having on the organization (operational and financial)?
- What is prompting the need to invest in usability at this time?
  - Loss of market share?
  - Changes in regulatory or certifying requirements?
  - Desire to cut costs associated with EHR training, support and decreased productivity?
  - New technologies or processes that can yield tangible business benefits?
- How does the proposed project fit with the organization's current strategy?
- Why should it be done now and what will happen if nothing is done?

Objectives. What will the usability project achieve? Write objectives using the SMART format where SMART is an acronym for *specific, measureable, achievable, relevant* and *time-bound*. Avoid using terms in objectives that are not measureable such as improve, help and optimize.

Options. This section describes the different options or alternatives that can be used to address the business need and how well each option achieves the desired objectives. Remember to include options that maintain the status quo, describing what will happen if no action is taken. The option to improve usability and what can be expected should also be included.

Include criteria for measuring each option for comparison purposes. Financial impact may include reduction in costs, new revenue or increased profit margin. Operational impact may include increased productivity, increased user satisfaction and decreased error rates. The business plan must describe why these are significant to the organization at this time.

The option to improve usability can be broken down into phases by improving usability during the lifecycle or post-implementation, the latter of which is not recommended due to significantly increased costs and other issues related to unnecessary repetition of design, build, and test plus increased costs associated with training, implementation, stabilization, adoption, productivity and safety. Because executives reading the business case may be unfamiliar with usability, it is recommended that you detail these points to avoid distractions away from the main points.

Scope. The scope describes the boundaries of the project including what will be included and what will be excluded. Identification of business areas, people, processes and technology that will be affected should be identified and described.

Governance Structure. The governance structure describes who will provide oversight of the project, ultimately ensuring its success. Identification of key stakeholders including their current roles and responsibilities should be outlined, along with short descriptions of how they are expected to contribute to the usability project.

Project Milestones. A high-level outline of the timetable by key milestones and dates should be included. Items to be included are project charter, project plan, completion and review, project kickoff, phases of the project and completion. If you lack experience in project estimating, be aware that aggressive timelines seem like a good idea when you are pitching your idea, but they feel very different once the "meter is running."

Cost-Benefit Analysis. This is a critical section of the business plan. Expected costs related to the proposed usability project should be described and outlined on an annualized basis. Similar to the costs, the benefits targeted to be derived from the EHR usability project for the organization should be outlined as cost savings or revenue generation. Placing the cost-benefit analysis in a table can readily summarize key information for the readers. An example is provided in Table 6-1. Managers who would lose resources or budget should be asked to sign off on the items for which they would be responsible.

The example provided for reducing support calls might be similar to that found in a hospital setting. Think about the volume of support calls EHR vendors receive related to usability and the savings increase substantially.

Table 6-1: Cost-Benefit Analysis

Item and Definition	Calculation	Annualized Savings
Reduction in development costs: Decrease in time to complete project		
Reduction in development time: Decrease in time to market from 12 months to 9 months		
Increased user productivity: Decrease in average time to order lab from 3 minutes to 2 minutes		
Reduction in training costs: Decrease in time to learn from 10 hours to 6 hours		
Reduction in support costs: Decrease help desk calls by 25%	Number of calls to help desk per year = 365,000 Average length of calls = 5 minutes (.17 hours) Number of calls per hour = 12 calls Reduction in calls = 25% Average help desk staff salary = $17.00/hour Cost of help desk support before usability improvement = 365,000 call / year x $17 per hour / 12 calls per hour = $517,083/80 annually Savings due to reduced calls = (365,000*17*12)*0.25 = $129,270.80 Cost of usability improvement = $25,000	$104,270.80

Funding Plan. The plan outlines the sources of funding for the project and how much each will provide. The plan should also include how funding will be delivered to the project, in increments over time or upfront.

Dependencies. Dependencies to the project should be identified as people, processes and technology. For example, will the project be dependent on a usability expert being available during a certain time period or will the project depend on a software application to be completed?

Constraints. These include things that must be considered for the usability project that cannot be changed. These can include regulatory requirements, technology limitations and deadlines.

Potential Risks and Mitigation Strategies. It is important to identify key risks that might prevent the ability to meet project requirements, deliver on time and stay within budget. Risks may include resource constraints, hard deadlines, availability of usability expertise and technology issues. The probability of occurrence, potential impact, actions to mitigate risks and contingency plans should be included.

Project Controls. Project controls include issues management, change management, quality assurance and user acceptance. How will issues related to scope, deadlines, human resources, cost variances and deliverables be handled and monitored? What change control process will be used? How will quality assurance be performed? And how will user acceptance testing be performed?

Communication Plan. The communication plan outlines *who* sends and receives communications, *what* communication is sent and received, *when* each communication should be delivered, *why* or the purpose of the communication, and *how* or what method is best used to communicate in each situation.

Approvals. Who needs to approve the business plan? Sign-offs should be considered for executive sponsor(s), project sponsor(s), project manager, quality and risk management and communications management. For vendors, marketing should be included; for buyers, chief clinicians should be included.

> *"When we adapt a traditional cost-justification analysis technique to making a business case for investing in usability services, it is in many cases surprisingly easy to make a very compelling case that shows a remarkable ROI on the cost of our services."*[15]

CONCLUSION

Avoid getting stuck in the emergency department of usability. Choose to avoid the usability flaws that are costly to vendors, buyers, users and patients. To chart this course requires knowledge not only of usability but also an appreciation of the multiple benefits that can be gained by all with improved usability of EHRs. The next chapter, Chapter 7, describes the future of EHR usability.

REFERENCES

1. Weinschenk S. *Usability: A Business Case*. Fairfield, IA: Human Factors International, April 7, 2005.

2. McCann E. EHR users ditching systems, trading up. *Health Care IT News*. July 23, 2013. Available at: http://goo.gl/JY4JZ. Accessed July 23, 2013.

3. Hadley B. Clean, cutting-edge UI design cuts McAfee support calls by 90%. *SoftwareCEO*. July 6, 2004. Available at: http://goo.gl/1WbhfT. Accessed July 24, 2103.

4. Boehm B. Software engineering. *IEEE Transactions*. 1976; 100(25):1226-1241.

5. Boehm B. A view of 20th and 21st century software engineering. International Conference on Software Engineering, May 26, 2006; Shangai, China. Available at: http://goo.gl/uKupBc. Accessed July 28, 2013.

6. Perna G. KLAS: athenahealth, Epic lead the way for ambulatory EMR usability. *Healthc Inform*. June 6, 2013. Available at: http://goo.gl/Quql3M. Accessed July 28, 2013.

7. Easthaugh SR. The total cost of EHR ownership. *Healthc Financ Manage*. 2013; 66-70.

8. Industry Usability Reporting Project Steering Committee, National Institute of Standards and Technology. Don't neglect usability in the total cost of ownership. *Communications of the ACM*. 2004; 47(7):11.

9. Butow E. *User Interface Design for Mere Mortals*. Upper Saddle River, NJ: Pearson Education, 2007.

10. Bias RG, Mayhew DJ, eds. *Cost-Justifying Usability: An Update for the Internet Age*. San Francisco, CA: Elsevier, 2005.

11. Wilson CE, Rosenbaum S. Categories of return on investment and their practical implications. In: Bias RG, Mayhew DJ, eds. *Cost-Justifying Usability: An Update for the Internet Age*. San Francisco, CA: Elsevier, 2005, 215-263.

12. Marcus A. Return on investment for usable user-interface design: Examples and statistics. Available at: http://goo.gl/OpjcJA. Accessed August 9, 2013.

13. Nielsen J, Berger JM, Gilutz S, et al. *Return on Investment (ROI) for Usability*. Fremont, CA: Nielsen Norman Group; 2003.

14. Rajanen M, Iivari N. Usability cost-benefit analysis: How usability became a curse word? In: Baranauskas C, et al. eds. INTERACT 2007, LNCS 4663, Part II, 511-524.

15. Mayhew DJ. Make a stronger business case for usability. *TechSmith*. 2008. Available at: http://goo.gl/pMdAZz. Accessed July 30, 2013.

16. Bevan N. Cost benefits framework and case studies. In: Bias RG, Mayhew DJ, eds. *Cost-Justifying Usability: An Update for the Internet Age*. San Francisco, CA: Elsevier, 2005.

17. Usability Net. Calculate the benefits of usability – for your business. Available at: http://goo.gl/EcmFDh. Accessed July 28, 2013.

18. Norman DA. *The Design of Everyday Things*. New York: Basic Books, 2002.

19. Harrington L. Usability of the electronic health record. *Health Aff*. 2013; 32(3):629.

20. Agency for Healthcare Research and Quality Electronic Health Record Usability: Interface Design Considerations (AHRQ Publication No. 09(10)-0091-2-EF, October 2009.

21. Healthcare Information Management and Systems Society. Promoting Usability in Health Organizations: Initial Steps and Progress Toward a Healthcare Usability Maturity Model. 2011. Available at: http://goo.gl/Y3eM28. Accessed August 17, 2013.

22. Saitwal H, Feng X, Walji M, et al. Assessing performance of an Electronic Health Record (EHR) using cognitive task analysis. *Int J Med Inform*. 2010; 79(7):501-506.

23. Jakob Nielsen's Alertbox. 10 Usability Heuristics for User Interface Design. January 1, 1995. Available at: http://www.nngroup.com/articles/ten-usability-heuristics/. Accessed August 19, 2013.

24. Zachary W, Neville K, Fowlkes J. Human total cost of ownership: The penny foolish principle at work. *IEEE Intell Syst*. 2007; 22(2):88-92.

CHAPTER 7

The Future of EHR Usability

"Technology is only good if it really fades away and it does something that humans actually want to do . . . "
— Jack Dorsey, Twitter Co-Founder and Square CEO

Just as we have seen bookstores, movie theatres, shops and banks fade into the background, replaced by a small app interface on a smart phone, so too will we see EHRs fade into the background. With increasing digitization of human data, we will see data entry by clinicians fade away. We will see touchless EHR interfaces move into view. And we will see a very diverse population of consumers, in terms of health literacy, languages and access, dependent upon EHR usability in order to make the best healthy choices.

FUTURE OF EHR USABILITY

Undoubtedly the biggest thing to happen in EHR usability will be *personalized usability*. We see a hint of that today with physicians using personalized electronic order sets and smart forms for documentation. We see a bigger hint of it with smart phones and apps, whereby people use the apps they need and can also read a book, watch a movie, shop and more. An even better hint of this personalization is seen in websites that "learn" from the people who are using them, offering back suggestions based on past choices.

Personal usability recognizes that each person's needs, context and likes impact their usability.[1] This will require EHR applications that learn from users' experiences and can reliably predict users' preferences. Just as machine learning will be scouring EHR data algorithmically to identify patients at risk in order to suggest courses of action, machine learning will scour EHR user behavior to suggest courses of action that make the EHR more usable, useful and satisfactory to users.

FUTURE OF EHR USABILITY EVALUATION

EHR usability evaluation will spread as larger numbers of people come to appreciate its relationship to safety, productivity, costs, and satisfaction. The impact of EHR usability will gain new meaning as we move further into pay for performance and providers continue to look for reimbursement improvements and cost-cutting measures.

Usability research evaluation will dramatically increase as the number of informatics researchers being educated continues to increase. To realize the benefits of these valuable resources will require significantly greater research funding specific to EHR usability.

EHR usability evaluation as a science will become more predictive and prescriptive about how to create good usability for individual users, workflow and contexts. Usability science is better today at identifying what does *not* work. In the future, it will further develop to tell us what works best.

FUTURE OF EHR USERS

Clinician EHR users will be less involved in data entry and more involved as data users. The challenges of EHRs today will fade away as predictive and prescriptive analytics take front and center stage in their view. Presentation of these analytics to users will also require excellent usability to enable them to interpret information appropriately and to intervene promptly.

The future of EHR usability will evolve to meet the needs of diversity. Users will increasingly involve more patients and families as people become more accountable for their health. There is also a growing concern about EHR-related healthcare disparities among certain populations of patients, specifically people with lower socioeconomic status and/or limited English proficiency, individuals older than age 65, people with disabilities, and racial and ethnic minorities.[2] Without excellent usability, these EHR users are at risk for reduced accessibility, as well as limited comprehension and understanding of information in the EHR inevitably causing suboptimal adoption and use among these high-risk patients.[2]

CONCLUSION

"The first rule of any technology used in a business is that automation applied to an efficient operation will magnify the efficiency. The second is that automation applied to an inefficient operation will magnify the inefficiency." —Bill Gates

It would be incredibly misleading to suggest that the recipe for EHR usability is complete. The confluence of so many complex and confounding fields—legal, regulatory, information sciences, logistics, quality, safety, education, customer service, finance, and of course, medicine and its allied sciences, to name some of the prominent ones—makes the field of healthcare incredibly complex. It is no wonder then that EHRs are some of the most complicated systems on the planet. And if you had to bet, would you be willing to put a chip on the square that says EHRs will become less complicated based on their current trajectory? Not likely. So given that EHRs already play a major role in our healthcare, it is tantamount that the benefits of usability are leveraged to make today's and tomorrow's EHRs better. We must move past the foibles and inefficiencies to create EHRs that effortlessly give providers the information they need, when they need it, and in the way they need it. Vendors must innovate, relentlessly pursuing excellent usability and leaving paper-based electronic designs in the rearview mirror. Researchers must advance the science and validate innovations to ensure their safety and effectiveness when they reach the practice setting. Clinicians must demand no less than excellence in usability to ease their journey to provide excellent patient care. Health IT must be a trusted partner to clinicians, following sound principles of usability knowing that a human life lost because of a preventable usability mistake is an enduring tragedy. Government agencies, professional organizations and others must provide sufficient funding for usability research, as the partnership of clinicians, heath IT and EHRs is the foundation of healthcare transformation, a transformation that must happen for healthcare to deliver on its promise of better outcomes for all. We must all work together, and we must all make usability a top priority. And we must do so now.

REFERENCES

1. Kay J. A test-first view of usability. *Interact Comput*. 2009; 21:347-349.

2. Gibbons MC, Lowry SZ, Quinn MT. Human Factors Guidance to Prevent Healthcare Disparities with the Adoption of EHRs (NISTIR 7769). National Institute of Standards and Technology. April 7, 2011.

Additional Resources

GOVERNMENT RESOURCES

Agency for Healthcare Research and Quality (AHRQ)

EHR Usability Toolkit: A Background Report on Usability and Electronic Health Records, 2011, http://goo.gl/z4VK7z

Electronic Health Record Usability: Vendor Practices and Perspectives, 2010, http://goo.gl/baS6J3

Electronic Health Record Usability: Interface Design Considerations, 2009, http://goo.gl/wMXVMr

Electronic Health Record Usability: Evaluation and Use Case Framework, 2009, http://goo.gl/pc2tNd

National Center for Cognitive Informatics & Decision Making
https://sbmi.uth.edu/nccd/

National Institute of Standards and Technology

Toward a Shared Approach for Ensuring Patient Safety with Enhanced Workflow Design for Electronic Health Records – Summary of the Workshop, 2013, http://goo.gl/rAieSF

A Human Factors Guide to Enhance EHR Usability of Critical User Interactions when Supporting Pediatric Patient Care, 2012, http://goo.gl/fqxcKt

Technical Evaluation, Testing and Validation of the Usability of Electronic Health Records Literature, 2012, http://goo.gl/LPi9ls

Customized Common Industry Format Template for Electronic Health Record Usability Testing, 2011, http://goo.gl/Od0AoG

Human Factors Guidance to Prevent Healthcare Disparities with the Adoption of EHRs, 2011, http://goo.gl/7jaFEJ

NIST Guide to the Processes Approach for Improving the Usability of Electronic Health Records, 2010, http://goo.gl/xQTjRL

US Department of Health & Human Services, National Cancer Institute
www.usability.gov (multiple usability resources)

USABILITY-SPECIFIC PROFESSIONAL ORGANIZATIONS

User Experience Professional Association (UXPA) (formerly Usability Professionals Association—UPA)
www.uxpa.org

Human Factors and Ergonomics Society (HFES)
www.hfes.org

Human Factors and Ergonomics Society, Europe Chapter
www.hfes-europe.org

PROFESSIONAL ASSOCIATION RESOURCES

Healthcare Information and Management Systems Society (HIMSS)
http://goo.gl/psdCLc
http://goo.gl/pOGpZR

HIMSS Usability Maturity Model
http://goo.gl/2prsfI

American Medical Informatics Association (AMIA)
http://goo.gl/tNq9X4

INTERNATIONAL

European Union
www.usabilitynet.org (multiple usability resources)

International Standards Organization (ISO)
Ergonomics of human-system interaction: Human-centered design for interactive systems (ISO 9241-210)

OTHER

Nielsen Norman Group
www.nngroup.com (formerly www.useit.com)

Usability Resources
www.usabilityresources.net

STATEMENTS BY PROFESSIONAL ASSOCIATIONS

American Medical Informatics Association
Enhancing patient safety and quality of care by improving usability of electronic health record systems: recommendations from AMIA, 2012
http://goo.gl/KpOby1

American Medical Association

Health IT Policy Committee, Certification/Adoption Workgroup, 2011
http://goo.gl/Ybx8uG

Index

f = figure entry
t = table entry